Birds of Big Bend National Park and Vicinity

Lucifer Hummingbirds at Mountain Sage

Birds of
Big Bend National Park
and Vicinity

by ROLAND H. WAUER

Paintings by
Howard Rollin and Anne Pulich

UNIVERSITY OF TEXAS PRESS
AUSTIN AND LONDON

This book is published with the assistance of the Big Bend Natural History Association, a co-operative association of the National Park Service.

Library of Congress Cataloging in Publication Data

Wauer, Roland H
    Birds of Big Bend National Park and vicinity.

    Bibliography: p.
    1. Birds—Big Bend National Park. 2. Birds—
Texas—Big Bend Region. I. Title.
QL684.T4W38   598.2'9764'932   72-7133
ISBN 0-292-70705-3

Composition by G&S Typesetters, Austin
Printing by R. R. Donnelley & Sons Company, Chicago

CONTENTS

Preface ix
The Big Bend Country 3
Bird Finding 31
Annotated List of Species 53
    Loons: Family Gaviidae, 54
    Grebes: Family Podicipedidae, 54
    Pelicans: Family Pelecanidae, 56
    Cormorants: Family Phalacrocoracidae, 56
    Herons and Bitterns: Family Ardaidae, 56
    Storks: Family Ciconiidae, 60
    Ibises and Spoonbills: Family Threskiornithidae, 60
    Swans, Geese, and Ducks: Family Anatidae, 61
    American Vultures: Family Cathartidae, 68
    Hawks, Eagles, and Harriers: Family Accipitridae, 69
    Ospreys: Family Pandionidae, 77
    Caracaras and Falcons: Family Falconidae, 77
    Quails, Pheasants, and Peacocks: Family Phasianidae, 80
    Cranes: Family Gruidae, 82
    Rails, Gallinules, and Coots: Family Rallidae, 83
    Plovers: Family Charadriidae, 85
    Woodcocks, Snipes, and Sandpipers: Family Scolopacidae, 86
    Avocets and Stilts: Family Recurvirostridae, 90
    Phalaropes: Family Phalaropodidae, 91
    Gulls and Terns: Family Laridae, 91
    Pigeons and Doves: Family Columbidae, 92
    Cuckoos, Roadrunners, and Anis: Family Cuculidae, 96

Barn Owls: Family Tytonidae, *97*
Typical Owls: Family Strigidae, *98*
Goatsuckers: Family Caprimulgidae, *101*
Swifts: Family Apodidae, *103*
Hummingbirds: Family Trochilidae, *103*
Kingfishers: Family Alcedinidae, *109*
Woodpeckers: Family Picidae, *110*
Tyrant Flycatchers: Family Tyrannidae, *113*
Larks: Family Alaudidae, *122*
Swallows: Family Hirundinidae, *122*
Jays, Ravens, and Nutcrackers: Family Corvidae, *126*
Titmice, Verdins, and Bushtits: Family Paridae, *128*
Nuthatches: Family Sittidae, *130*
Creepers: Family Certhiidae, *131*
Wrens: Family Troglodytidae, *131*
Mockingbirds and Thrashers: Family Mimidae, *135*
Thrushes, Bluebirds, and Solitaires: Family Turdidae, *138*
Gnatcatchers and Kinglets: Family Sylviidae. *142*
Pipits: Family Motacillidae, *144*
Waxwings: Family Bombycillidae, *145*
Silky Flycatchers: Family Ptilogonatidae, *145*
Shrikes: Family Laniidae, *146*
Starlings: Family Sturnidae, *147*
Vireos: Family Vireonidae, *147*
Wood Warblers: Family Parulidae, *152*
Weaver Finches: Family Ploceidae, *167*
Meadowlarks, Blackbirds, and Orioles: Family Icteridae, *168*
Tanagers: Family Thraupidae. *180*
Grosbeaks, Buntings, Finches, and Sparrows:
    Family Fringillidae, *182*
Birds of Uncertain Occurrence, *205*
Bibliography, *211*
Index of Common Names, *217*

ILLUSTRATIONS

Lucifer Hummingbirds at Mountain Sage . Frontispiece
Colima Warbler 2
The Rio Grande at Santa Elena Canyon . . . 5
Tornillo Creek 6
The Chisos Mountains, Western Slope 7
Floodplain near Castolon 9
Pond at Rio Grande Village 10
Cottonwood Grove at Rio Grande Village . . . 13
Government Spring 15
Chihuahuan Desert Lowlands 16
Desert Arroyo 18
Chinograss on Lower Chisos Foothills 20
Sotol along Dodson Trail 21
Blue Creek Canyon 22
Woodland of Pinyon, Junipers, and Oaks . . . 24
Chaparral at Laguna Meadow 25
Boot Canyon 27
Ponderosa Pines in Pine Canyon 28
Rio Grande Village Nature Trail 30
Birds of the Floodplain 41
Birds of the Arroyos and the Shrub Desert . . . 43
Birds of the Grassland 44
Birds of the Pinyon-Juniper-Oak Woodlands . . . 46
Birds of the Cypress-Pine-Oak Woodlands . . . 47
Wintering Birds 48
Map of Big Bend National Park . . . . . fol. 32

PREFACE

The Big Bend Country is one of those special "must visit" places for bird watchers. It is one of a handful of localities in the southern latitudes of the United States that represents choice birding. Places like the Everglades, Aransas, Rockport, Ramsey Canyon, the Chiricahuas, and the Chisos sooner or later show up on every birder's calendar. Big Bend National Park offers a wider variety of birds—385 species have been recorded—than any other national park.

This book is designed for the nature lover who has a special interest in birds. Its intent is to help the visiting birder find the particular birds he may wish to see. It is a "where-to-go-to-find-what" book, not a field guide to bird identity. This book should be a companion to the popular field guides that more than likely are already part of your library: Roger Tory Peterson's *A Field Guide to the Birds of Texas*, and *Birds of North America*, by Chandler Robbins and others. *Birds of Big Bend National Park and Vicinity* should be used as a guidebook to bird finding while you are visiting the Big Bend Country.

This book has been written to satisfy two worlds: that of the ornithologist, who may be most interested in statistics and records, and that of the bird watcher, who may watch birds simply for the sheer thrill of seeing an old friend or making a new one.

BIRD STUDY IN THE BIG BEND

The first ornithological investigation within the Big Bend Country was by a party from the United States Biological Survey in 1901. During May, June, and July of that year, Harry C. Oberholser, Vernon Bailey, and Louis Agassiz Fuertes did extensive field work throughout the area. Oberholser summarized the more important findings in 1902, Fuertes published on the Harlequin Quail in 1903, and Bailey reported on the expedition's total findings in 1905. In 1904, Thomas H. Montgomery collected birds around Alpine and southward to the Chisos Mountains between June 13 and July 6. He reported his findings in a paper on the "summer resident" birds of Brewster County in 1905. And the following year, John K. Strecker briefly visited the Big Bend area in April and May.

This early period of activity was followed by one in which expeditions to this remote section of the United States were discouraged. The Mexican Revolution caused considerable unrest along the Mexican border. For the next twenty years, except for Austin Paul Smith's visit to the Davis Mountains from September 2 to October 16, 1916, the only ornithologists to visit the Big Bend area were those associated with the military. Frank B. Armstrong was one of those who collected birds for Col. John E. Thayer in May, 1913, and in January and February, 1914. George E. Maxon, a member of the Texas National Guard, was stationed at Boquillas, Terlingua, and Lajitas, and collected bird eggs throughout the area during 1916. Maxon published his findings in two papers that same year.

It was not until 1928 that additional ornithological research was instigated within the Big Bend. That year, Josselyn Van Tyne and Frederick M. and Helen T. Gaige surveyed the country from Alpine to the top of Emory Peak between June 8 and August 7. The Gaige–Van Tyne party spent considerable time at Glenn Springs, San Vicente, Hot Springs, and Boquillas. They even reached Boot Canyon, where Frederick Gaige collected a Colima Warbler on July 20. The specimen represented the first for the United States and only the twelfth known specimen of this warbler. Van Tyne reported the most important data obtained on this expedition in 1929. The opportunity to find a new breeding bird for the United States prompted Van Tyne to return in 1932. His second visit, when he was accompanied by Max M. Peet and Edouard C. Jacot, lasted from April 26 through June 22. Their success was published in Van Tyne's 1936 paper, "The Discovery of the Nest of the Colima Warbler (*Vermivora crissalis*)."

News of their ornithological discoveries soon attracted other biologists to the area. In the spring of 1933, George Miksch Sutton, John B. Semple, and Albert C. Lloyd spent more than a month within the Big Bend. Several days were spent around Marathon, Castolon, Hot Springs, and Boquillas, but visits to Juniper and Pine canyons were accomplished before they turned north to the Del Norte and Glass mountains. Sutton published a fascinating account of this trip, "An Expedition to the Big Bend Country," in 1935, and a chapter of his 1936 book, *Birds in the Wilderness*, is devoted to this and a second trip to the Big Bend in 1935.

At about this same time, considerable interest was being expressed by concerned Texans about a national park within the lower Big Bend Country. This interest prompted the National Park Service to send biologists to the area to investigate its potential. Ben H. Thompson surveyed the wildlife for the Park Service in 1934, and several additional biologists were sent into the area during 1935 and 1936: James O. Stevenson, Walter A. Weber, Tarleton F. Smith, and Adrey E. Borell. Stevenson, accompanied by Van Tyne, who was returning for this third visit, reported his findings in 1935. Smith submitted a report on his studies in 1936, and Borell reported on her findings in 1936 and 1938. In addition, Roy W. Quillin, an independent ornithologist, published a note on his visit to the lower Big Bend Country in 1935. And in 1937, Herbert Brandt and associates spent the first half of May studying birds within the Chisos Mountains. He reported on new races of the White-breasted Nuthatch and Hutton's Vireo in 1938, and summarized his experiences in *Texas Bird Adventures* in 1940. This book offers an interesting account of his birding as well as an early description of the country itself.

By 1937, sufficient information on the birdlife of the area was available for Van Tyne and Sutton to collaborate on a comprehensive analysis of the avifauna in "The Birds of Brewster County, Texas." This 120-page paper, published by the University of Michigan Press, was based upon 425 man-days of field work by the authors and the combined information of earlier researchers. They reported a total of 215 species of birds for Brewster County.

Big Bend National Park was established on June 12, 1944. That congressional act resulted in the complete protection of all animals and plants and the historic and geographic features within the 708,221-acre park. It began a new era. For the first time since cattle were driven into the lush grasslands of the Chisos Mountains in 1885, the plant life was allowed to begin its own slow recovery. More than forty-thousand head of stock, mostly goats and sheep, had been removed from the area in 1943 and 1944.

In an attempt to monitor the natural recovery of the park's plant communities, vegetative transects were established during the mid-1940's. Walter P. Taylor, Walter B. McDougall, and William B. Davis completed a "Preliminary Report on an Ecological Survey of Big Bend National Park" in 1944, and by the mid-1950's an ecological survey team from Texas A&M University was stationed within the park. Team member Richard D. Porter resided there from June, 1957, through early August, 1959. During that time he collected a large series of birds, many of which were deposited in the Big Bend study collection or at Texas A&M. Several of the members of this team kept records of the park's birdlife, and a number of reports were eventually published; Keith L. Dixon and O. Charles Wallmo published a series of bird records in 1956, and Dixon reported on desert shrub birds in 1959.

In 1956, Col. L. R. Wolfe summarized all the state's bird records in his *Check-list of the Birds of Texas*. This publication is still the most complete listing of the birds of Texas.

Also in the mid-1950's, several Park Service employees began to record their bird observations. Park Ranger Dick Youse recorded several important observations from May, 1955, through September, 1956. Harold Brodrick became the park's first park naturalist in December, 1955, and, until his departure in October, 1961, he maintained an excellent series of bird records. Brodrick prepared a "Check-list of the Birds of Big Bend National Park" in 1960. This mimeographed list included 236 species of birds that had been reported for the park. The list included the records of other Big Bend residents—Pete Koch, John Palmer, Harold Schaafsma, Rod Broyles, and Pat Miller —as well as many park visitors who had thoughtfully sent their sightings to the park naturalist for park files. Brodrick's checklist was revised in 1966 by C. Philip Allen and Anne LeSassier, who added several important records and brought the list to 241 species.

My arrival in Big Bend National Park in August, 1966, allowed me the opportunity to visit several strategic locations many times all twelve months of the year. For the first time, the study of the birds of Big Bend began to show some continuity. In spite of the fact that the area had had visits from some of the finest field ornithologists in the world, their records had not been thoroughly analyzed for a publication on birds.

Field trips were taken one to four times a week at Rio Grande Village and the Chisos Basin. Boot Canyon, Castolon, and Laguna Meadow were surveyed regularly; and occasional visits to many other places were made throughout the period of August, 1966, through October, 1971. An estimated total of 3,589 manhours in field research and more than 400 hours in analysis of avian records and the park's vegetation have been spent. In addition to my efforts, many, many birders and ornithologists were kind enough to allow access to their findings. If it were not for these helpful individuals, this book would certainly not include as many observations as it does. I gratefully thank Alexander Sprunt, Jr., Alexander Sprunt IV, and Walter Sieckert, who reported their observations in 1949; John and Margaret Galley, Orrin and Ethel Letson, and Alexander Sprunt, Jr., in 1950; Edward Chalif, Irby Davis, Guy Emerson, Roger Tory Peterson, Clara and Harold Spore, Margaret and Alexander Sprunt, Jr., and John H. Dick in 1951; Dorothy E. Snyder in 1954; Jack Burgess in 1956; Louise and Henry Hoffman in

1957; Thompson G. Marsh, Theodore M. Sperry, and Gladys C. Galliger in 1960; Robert C. Stein, and Warren and Bobby Pulich in 1961; Joe Marshall in 1962; Joseph and Harriet Woolfenden, Benjamin and Joanne Trimble, John H. Groet, Adele West, and C. Philip Allen in 1963; Mr. and Mrs. Roy B. Hipple, Mr. and Mrs. C. Edgar Bedell, R. J. and Lola Walston, Hoyt and Gail McKerley, B. J. Rose, Paul R. Julian, Raymond and Mona Fleetwood, and Peter and Ruth Isleib in 1964; Capt. E. B. Hurlbert in 1965; I. R. Sauvageau, Jon C. Barlow, Carl J. Swenson, M. Kent Rylander, Clarence Cottam, Mr. and Mrs. C. Edgar Bedell, John Hardy, and Mr. and Mrs. Gerald Harding in 1966; Russ and Marion Wilson, Helga Cernicek, Bill Schultz, Hanlon, McCarroll, Meyer, Kuehn, Rowe, John and Ethelyne Bizilo, Mrs. L. Q. Reese, Dave Easterla, Dick Nelson, Fred R. Gehlbach, Frances Williams, and John S. Weske in 1967; Ele and Flew Lewis, Robert B. Payne, R. L. West, Stanley Speck, W. J. Wayne, Karl Weber, Robert Thompson, Paul and Martha Whitson, Patricia Snider, David Simon, Barbara Ribble, Ruth Black, David Wolf, and Joe W. Taylor in 1968; Jim Cameron, D. L. Steed, R. Moore, Mr. and Mrs. Frank Eastman, Kay Curtiss, Mr. and Mrs. A. J. Angante, George R. Shier, Robert Rothstein, Susan and Richard Block, Ty and Julie Hotchkiss, Charles E. Newell, Terry Hall, Doyle and Helen Peckham, H. Cook Anderson, Bob Smith, and Dr. and Mrs. R. C. Smith in 1969; Terry C. Maxwell, Mr. and Mrs. Murl Deusing, Bert and Millie Schaughency, Terry Thormin, Monty Brigham, Charles Bender, Ty and Julie Hotchkiss, David Wolf, James Middleton, H. Lee Watson, John MacDonald, and Tom Myres in 1970; and Mrs. James Owen, Catherine and Carroll Pickard, Steve Williams, Dr. and Mrs. Glenn Stevens, Bert and Millie Schaughency, Charles and Ella Newell, R. Loehning, H. H. and R. C. Axtell, Jim Tucker, Harold Baxter, Ted Parker, Harold Morrin, Joel Greenberg, Jeffrey Sanders, Lena McBee, and Richard Webster in 1971.

Thanks are also due to a few individuals who have given me special help during my research and preparation of this book. I wish to thank Mr. Howard Rollin of Weldona, Colorado. Mr.

Rollin has made a special series of water colors of the birds of the Big Bend National Park and has kindly given his permission for their reproduction here. The frontispiece—a pair of Lucifer Hummingbirds at Mountain Sage—was painted by Mrs. Anne Pulich. Anne has painted numerous birds of Texas, and her beautiful paintings are seen throughout the state. I also wish to thank Big Bend National Park superintendents Perry Brown, Luther T. Peterson, Jr., and Joe F. Carithers for consenting to the project and permitting its continuance. Dr. James Scudday and Dr. Barton H. Warnock, Sul Ross State University, gave me considerable encouragement and permitted me to utilize this material for a Master's thesis. Pete Koch, chairman of the Board of Directors of the Big Bend Natural History Association, gave the project a push with the proposal of financing its publication by the association. I thank Dr. Allan R. Phillips for his abundant ideas and inspirations regarding birds and their ecology and for identification of specimens; Dr. Richard C. Banks and Dr. Ned K. Johnson, National Museum and Museum of Vertebrate Zoology, for specimen identifications; Dr. Keith A. Arnold for preparation of a list of Big Bend specimens at Texas A&M University; Dr. George M. Sutton for suggestions on the Preface; Frances Williams for help in obtaining out-of-print publications and also for her enthusiasm and interest in West Texas birds; Pansy Espy and Clay and Jody Miller for their help in obtaining information on the Davis Mountains and Jeff Davis County; Dr. Charles B. Hunt for suggestions on geological statements; Noberto Ortega for help with supplies and transportation; Sam Bishop for help with the aerial study of the Rio Grande floodplain; Ruth Jessen, who read the manuscript for grammatical corrections; and Roger Siglin, Jim Court, and Dave Easterla for their continuous interest and support during their residency in Big Bend National Park.

And last, but certainly not least, my wife, Sharon, who read and typed the major portion of the manuscript, and for reasons that only "birds widows" can understand.

Birds of Big Bend National Park and Vicinity

Colima Warbler

The Big Bend Country

Half way between El Paso and Laredo, the Rio Grande makes a great southern bend into the Mexican states of Chihuahua and Coahuila. The river course follows the southeastern trend of mountains and basins until it reaches the confluence of the Rio Conchos, the ancestral river that formed the present Rio Grande Valley (Charles B. Hunt, personal communications). Below Presidio it cuts across the mountains and forms a huge bend as it flows toward the southeast, east, and northeast. It finally reaches other southeastern valleys that it follows to the sea. In its wake across the mountains lie gigantic canyons and impenetrable ridges. Lying within this great arc is a wild and remote area that has come to be known as the Texas Big Bend Country.

It takes little imagination to visualize the chaotic changes that led to Big Bend's creation. Today, almost every valley and mountain within the lower part of the Big Bend Country can be regarded as a classic geologic feature. Three great canyons have been cut through the tremendous layers of limestone that form high cliffs along three sides of the lower Big Bend. Between these high scarps is a forty-mile-wide trough that dropped downward in the geologic past. Rising out of the center of these lowlands is a mountain range that forms the southernmost montane area in the United States. These mountains—the Chisos—are the only contiguous mountain mass entirely within a national park.

A national park was established within this area in 1944. There are preserved more than 708,000 acres of desert and mountain landscape ranging from 1,800 to 7,835 feet elevation. The park's latitude is about the same as that of the mouth of the Mississippi River. Big Bend National Park may be considered the "showcase" of the Big Bend Country. Its lowlands contain some of the best examples in the world of the Chihuahuan Desert. The flora and fauna include numerous unique forms and many Mexican species that occur nowhere else in the United States. In fact, the Big Bend Country has often been considered to be more like that of Mexico than north of the border.

Two drainage systems develop below the Chisos and adjacent hills and mesas. Tornillo Creek drains the northern and eastern slopes of the Chisos, and Terlingua Creek drains its northwestern edge. With the Rio Grande, these intermittent creeks form a circle that completely surrounds the Chisos Mountains. Long and gradual eroded plains rise out of the drainages and form rolling hills alongside some of the sharp-rising mountain cliffs. A few deeply eroded canyons run from the desert lowlands to the tops of the highest peaks. The highlands of the igneous Chisos Mountains stand out in bold contrast to the surrounding lowlands.

Although the park may be considered to be the showcase of the Big Bend, it is by no means the only part of the greater Big Bend Country that is spectacular. Just north of the park, the Santiago Mountains form a long chain of flat-topped peaks that runs northwesterly to join the Del Nortes and continues northward to form a mountain mass larger and higher than the Chisos, the Davis Mountains. While the Chisos are bold and sudden, the Davis Mountains are rolling and full of valleys. It is perhaps this combination of differences that makes the Big Bend Country of Texas one of the most fascinating places in the world.

The Rio Grande curls its way through desert and mesa landscapes within the Texas Big Bend Country. Here it carves a magnificent canyon—Santa Elena—into the Mesa de Anguila of Mexico and the United States.

Tornillo Creek drains the northern and eastern portions of Big Bend National Park. The usually dry streambed can be a raging torrent following late-summer storms.

The Chisos Mountains, 7,835 feet in elevation, form the center of Big Bend National Park. This view is the western slope of the Chisos, taken from Rattlesnake Mountain.

All of Big Bend's topographical features—its peaks, hills, canyons, valleys, and flatlands—would be rather monotonous were it not for the vegetation that covers it. The plant life may be classified into defined zones according to plant types and abundance. These zones are of major importance to the bird watcher because each bird species prefers a particular vegetative place or habitat. Although soil types influence plant associations to a degree, climate affects them more significantly.

Precipitation, temperature, humidity, and days of cloud cover or direct sunlight all play an important part in the determination of types of vegetation. These factors are in turn influenced by elevation. The majority of Big Bend's precipitation comes during the six warm months from May through October; the greatest average for any single month has been recorded for September. Monthly rainfall varies from a trace to 6.5 inches. Average annual rainfall in the Chisos Basin is 15.72 inches; at Boquillas (Rio Grande Village), 10.13 inches. Snow is uncommon, but as much as 20 inches, undrifted, has been reported in the Chisos Basin. Snowfalls from a few to 8 inches are more common. The most arid section of the Big Bend Country is in the lowland area from Mariscal Mountain to Castolon, which may average 5 inches annually. The wettest areas are the mountain tops, where the annual precipitation may be 20 to 25 inches.

For about five months of the year, the mean daily maximums in the desert reach or exceed 100° Fahrenheit. Temperatures in the mountains average about 15 percent lower. During the cooler seven months, temperatures may drop below freezing at mid-elevations, while the lowlands along the river may never experience frost; the mountains may undergo below-freezing temperatures twenty to thirty times each winter.

PLANT COMMUNITIES

The Big Bend Country is truly a land of contrasts. There are few places where one can enjoy the pungent aroma of Creosotebush and travel less than a dozen miles to be dwarfed by stately

The Rio Grande floodplain offers suitable conditions for cotton-woods, willows, seepwillows, mesquites, and other water-loving plant species. In some places, such as this area near Castolon, the floodplain is broad, with extensive thickets of vegetation.

Ponds are few and far between along the Rio Grande. This one at Rio Grande Village offers yet another habitat on the river flood-plain.

Arizona Cypress, Ponderosa Pine, and Douglas Fir. It is because of this variety of plant life that the list of birds cannot be equaled anywhere in the United States, except for a few coastal localities. The determining factors of latitude, climate, and topography have provided at least five distinct plant communities and numerous associations.

The Floodplain and Arroyos

The Rio Grande forms a belt of greenery along its entire course. Floodplain vegetation exists wherever periodic flooding occurs. These areas may extend from a few feet to one-half mile from the river channel, except where sheer cliffs rise directly out of the riverbed. Adjacent arroyos and creeks may carry enough surface or ground water to produce an environment similar to that of the Rio Grande floodplain.

Common and Giant reeds grow along the banks so close to the river that they often form a protective shelter along the edge of the waterway. Other water-loving plants whose canopy may hang out over the river include the Lanceleaf Cottonwood, willows, Honey Mesquite, Tamarisk, and Seepwillow. Just beyond this zone can be found Screwbean, Catclaw Acacia, Desertwillow, Wild Grape, Tree Tobacco, Common Buttonbush, and Arrow-weed. Heavy thickets of this environment may be found at a number of places along the river. The most accessible and best example of this plant association is along the lower portion of the Rio Grande Village Nature Trail. During late spring and summer, every bird known to nest in this type of habitat can usually be found there with little searching.

Ponds can be found in a few places, where the erratic Rio Grande has changed its channel or where man has dredged a pit. Tamarisk, Seepwillow, and Cowpen Daisy are early invaders to the eroded and moist soils. Common Cattail, Lanceleaf Cottonwood, and willows appear before long if there is sufficient water. The Rio Grande Village silt pond is deep enough to allow cattails to form a rather extensive marshy area. This type of community is rare within the park, but marshy areas exist at a number of places in the northern part of the Big Bend Country.

Beyond the zone of ponds and phreatophytes, a secondary group of plants with a slightly more xeric affinity can often be found. This is the arroyo environment, which may contain thickets of floodplain plants or hummocky thickets of mesquites and acacias. Old fields at Rio Grande Village, Hot Springs, Solis, and Castolon are example localities of this plant community in which mesquite is dominant. In fact, the composition of these areas may be 80 percent mesquite and only 20 percent other species, such as willows, Catclaw and Mescat acacias, Desertwillow, Guayacan, and pricklypear and Tasajillo cacti. Creosotebush is usually present along the edges of this association. Although the birds that nest in the arroyo environment are usually the same as in the floodplain environment next to the river, the avian compositions of these two associations are considerably different. Common nesting birds of the more humid floodplain include the Yellow-billed Cuckoo, Bell's Vireo, Yellow-breasted Chat, Cardinal, Blue Grosbeak, and Painted Bunting. Common nesting species of the mesquite bosques include the Lesser Nighthawk, Ash-throated Flycatcher, Verdin, Mockingbird, Black-tailed Gnatcatcher, Pyrrhuloxia, and House Finch. Species of each of these groups are uncommon nesting species within the opposite associations.

A number of specialized places occur along the floodplain. One of these is a grove of Lanceleaf Cottonwoods along the Santa Elena Crossing road, just below Castolon. This species of cottonwood has been almost totally exterminated in Texas by woodcutters and bulldozers. Breeding birds that frequent this grove today are about the same as can be found in the more arid parts of the floodplain. However, one cannot help but wonder what other species would use this habitat were it not so heavily abused by stock and woodcutters from across the river. In spite of National Park "protection" of this area, the Green Heron, Black Hawk, Wied's Crested Flycatcher, and other species must find suitable nesting places elsewhere.

Rio Grande Village and Cottonwood Campground are two

Just behind the store at Rio Grande Village is a cottonwood grove that offers an excellent birding area.

other unique areas. Native vegetation was cleared from these localities during the early part of the century. Cotton and other crops were raised on the cleared land until the areas came under Park Service control, Rio Grande Village in 1944 and Castolon in 1952. Parts of the flats were replanted with grass and fast-growing shade trees for the campground and picnic areas. At Rio Grande Village, the great number and variety of trees, along with an excellent spring that forms a "jungle" of floodplain vegetation at the Rio Grande Village Nature Trail, have succeeded in attracting a wide variety of resident birds as well as migrants. Rio Grande Village, because it is considerably larger than the Cottonwood area, is the best single place in the park where large numbers of birds may be found consistently.

Rio Grande Village encompasses more than seventy acres of flatlands at about 1,900 feet elevation. A one-hundred-site campground dominates the eastern half of the area. Thickets of mesquites and Guayacan encircle the camping sites, which are well shaded by a few native shrubs and trees and a number of exotics. There can be found native Lanceleaf Cottonwood, mesquites, Huisache, Guayacan, Squaw-bush, and Desertwillow growing alongside exotic Eastern Cottonwood, Smooth Sycamore, Live Oak, ash, Thornless Honeylocust, Tamarisk, and Eucalyptus over a Bermuda Grass lawn. North of the campground is an old field heavily overgrown with mesquites. Interspersed alongside and within the thickets of mesquite are grassy places and open, salty flats where little more than Pickle-weed, Alkali Sacaton, and Seaside Heliotrope occurs.

The Rio Grande Village Store is located near the center of the area. Behind the store is a small lake bordered by brushy areas to the north and a picnic and cottonwood area to the south and west. To the west, beyond a trailer court, are more old fields, a sandy hummocky area adjacent to the floodplain, and some rather dense Eastern Cottonwood groves. Just beyond the grove at the end of the road that runs west from the store is a silt pond that contains a dense cattail growth.

Tornillo and Terlingua creeks and a number of arroyos ex-

Government Spring is one of several small springs that surface within the grasslands surrounding the Chisos Mountains. In the background are Lost Mine Peak, Casa Grande, and Pulliam Peak.

The Chihuahuan Desert lowlands offer a rather stark environment, where specially adapted plants like cacti and Ocotillo are
dominant. This view was taken looking east toward the Chisos
Mountains from Maverick.

tend inland many miles and represent "fingers" of floodplain-arroyo vegetation. This plant association may persist within the drainages and at springs and seeps up into the grasslands to the base of the mountain woodlands. Although the dominant plant species usually are the same as in the lower arroyos adjacent to the river—mesquites, Catclaw Acacia, Guayacan, Desertwillow, and Seepwillow—several more xeric species begin to occur regularly. Beaked Yucca is quite common along the western end of the River Road, as well as within the lower slopes of the Dead Horse Mountains. Desert Hackberry, Fourwinged Saltbush, Desert Sumac, Javelina-Bush, Texas Persimmon, Desert Olive, and Wolfberry may be common along arroyos and at springs and seeps.

More than a dozen springs, numerous earthen tanks, and a few wells are scattered about within the shrub desert and grasslands. Glenn, Chilicotal, Government, and Grapevine springs, Paint Gap, Dagger Flat, and Willow tanks, and Dugout Wells are a few of these.

The Shrub Desert

The sheer cliffs that rise out of the Rio Grande riverbed contain only a sparse plant cover. The environment is closely tied into the ecology of the river and floodplain, but is included here because of the paucity of vegetation. At other places along the river the rocky slopes may be more gradual and offer a wider variety of plants. There the limestone slopes are often dominated by an assortment of succulents that includes Hechtia, Lechuguilla, Candelilla, and several cacti, particularly Blind Pricklypear.

The open flats beyond contain deeper soils and represent more typical examples of the shrub desert community. There is where the "barren desert" of the Big Bend can be found, the kind of desert that most first-time visitors expect to find. The Lechuguilla-Creosotebush-cactus association is characterized by succulents and small to medium-sized woody shrubs that are widely spaced. Lechuguilla, Creosotebush, Ocotillo, Blind

Desert arroyos offer the best habitats in which to find desert birds.
This arroyo lies near the River Road south of Glenn Springs.

Pricklypear, and Dog Cholla are the most common species; Fluffgrass, Torrey Yucca, Leather Stem, Candelilla, Longspine Pricklypear, and Tasajillo may be locally common.

Desert flats are never popular birding localities. Although some migrants pass through these areas and a few birds nest there, the adjacent arroyos, which contain vegetation more like that of the floodplain, are better places to find shrub desert birds than the open flats themselves. The vast area along the River Road, where open flats are interspersed with arroyos, is one of the better places to find typical desert birds.

The Grasslands

A fine intergradation of shrub desert and grassland vegetation occurs between 2,500 and 3,500 feet elevation. The grasslands begin where the more xeric desert plants become less numerous, and grasses become the dominant ground cover. This is the area where the open, "barren" flats give way to more grasses, semisucculents, and evergreen and deciduous shrubs.

Although the lower portion of the grasslands is very similar to the shrub desert, open flats become less extensive and gradually change to more rolling hills and knolls as elevation is increased. Closer to the mountains, washes lose their gradual relief and develop into distinct canyons. This is the zone of vegetation that made the Big Bend Country famous during the 1880's, when cattle was king and ranching was new to the Chisos. Large flats of Tobosa and Lochuguilla occur at the lower edges of the grassland community; Chinograss covers huge areas on the rolling foothills, often as a codominant with Creosotebush. Other common plants of the lower grasslands include Range Ratany, Guayacan, Leather Stem, Ocotillo, Ceniza. and Mariola.

Sotol may be present at 3.000 feet. but it does not become abundant until about 3,600 feet elevation, at the lower edge of the Sotol-grasslands that form a belt around the Chisos Mountains. This association extends into the lower limits of the woodlands and at a number of higher disjunct localities. Common

Chinograss is the dominant cover within the lower Chisos foothills. These hills lie just east of Dugout. The three major peaks in
the background are (*left to right*) Nuggent Mountain, Crown
Mountain, and Pummel Peak.

Sotol is a dominant plant of the higher grasslands. This view is southwest along the western end of the Dodson Trail.

Oak and other broadleaf trees are more common within drainages. Here in Blue Creek Canyon is a rather dense association of deciduous trees.

plants of the Sotol-grasslands include Sotol, Bull Muhly, Hairy and Black grama, Sideoats Grama, Blue Threeawn, Honey Mesquite, White-thorn Acacia, Cat's Claw Mimosa, Feather Dalea, Big Bend Agave, Desert Hackberry, Squaw-bush, Javelina-Bush, Texas Persimmon, and Skeletonleaf Goldeneye.

The Pinyon-Juniper-Oak Woodlands

Mountain woodlands of the Big Bend Country start at the upper edge of the Sotol-grasslands and cover most of the higher peaks and mesas. The woodland formation is a varied environment that may be divided into two distinct plant associations, the deciduous and the pinyon-juniper woodlands. The deciduous woodlands begin as low as 3,000 feet in a few of the washes within the Sotol-grasslands. This association of broadleaf shrubs and trees often intergrades with plants of the arroyo association. Honey Mesquite, Mescat Catclaw, and Desertwillow, which are common within the upper arroyos, also occur in pockets of more water-holding soils at about the same places that more xeric forms of the deciduous woodlands begin. Woodland species include the Black Walnut, Netleaf Hackberry, Apacheplume, Guayacan, Evergreen Sumac, Mexican Buckeye, Texas Persimmon, Common Bee-brush, and Skeletonleaf Goldeneye. The best examples of this habitat occur below Government Spring, in Cottonwood Wash, in lower Green Gulch, and in Panther, Oak Creek, and lower Blue Creek canyons.

Above the area of overlap, the deciduous woodlands are more like that of the higher canyons. Typical deciduous vegetation occurs in upper Green Gulch, Pine, Juniper, and Blue Creek canyons, and in lower and upper Boot Canyon. Dominant plants in these localities are the Gray, Emory, and Grave's oaks, Evergreen Sumac, Texas Madrone, Mountain Sage, and Scarlet Bouvardia. Bigtooth Maple occurs with this group in Boot Canyon.

The pinyon-juniper woodlands may form open, scattered stands of pine or may be evenly mixed with junipers and oaks. Almost pure stands of oaks and junipers occur along the lower

A woodland of pinyon, junipers, and oaks starts just above the grasslands and extends to the top of the Chisos Mountains.

Chaparral associations occur on several open slopes within the
Chisos Mountains. This one, along the northern end of Laguna
Meadow, is almost totally located on limy soils of an uplifted
block of Boquillas limestone.

fringes of the association; as elevation increases there are fewer junipers and more pines on the open slopes, and more oaks along the drainages and within the denser woodlands. Green Gulch offers the most accessible assortment of these habitats that are readily visible from the roadway. Heavier stands of pinyons and junipers can be found along the southeastern slopes of the Chisos Basin.

Dominant plants of the pinyon-juniper woodlands include the Mexican Pinyon, Red-berry, Drooping and Alligator junipers; Gray, Emory, and Grave's oaks; Evergreen and Fragrant sumacs, and a number of grasses that include Pinyon Ricegrass, Needlegrass, Plains Lovegrass, Bull Muhly, Blue Grama, and Arizona Threeawn. Other plant species found regularly in the pinyon-juniper woodlands are the Nolina, Big Bend Agave, Mountain Mahogany, Chisos Pricklypear, Claret-cup Cactus, Silktassel, Texas Madrone, and Mountain Sage.

In a few places between 4,500 and 6,500 feet elevation, vegetation associations of Dwarf Oak, Mountain Mahogany, Desert Ceonothus, Evergreen and Fragrant sumacs, and Silktassel form a chaparral-like growth. Examples of this Chisos chaparral community occur at the north end of Laguna Meadow, along the western slopes of the lower Basin, and in Juniper, Pine, and Blue Creek canyons. Because of its proximity to the woodland communities, and because I have found no species of birds restricted to this association within the Big Bend, the chaparral is considered only as part of the pinyon-juniper-oak woodlands.

The Cypress-Pine-Oak Woodlands

This is a "forest-edge" type of environment that exists in only a few of the highland canyons in the Chisos Mountains. Cypress-pine-oak woodlands occur within Boot Canyon and along the northern slope of Juniper Canyon below the East Rim. Boot Canyon runs northeast to southwest for about two and one-half miles. The relatively narrow, rocky canyon bottom is dominated by Arizona Cypress, Emory and Grave's oaks, Bigtooth Maple, Texas Madrone, Silktassel, and Mountain Sage.

Boot Canyon contains a woodland of pinyon and oaks in the open part of the canyon (*foreground*), and Arizona Cypress, pines, and oaks within the narrower canyon.

The largest stand of Ponderosa Pines in the park occurs along the north-facing slope of Pine Canyon. Band-tailed Pigeons, Acorn Woodpeckers, and White-breasted Nuthatches nest in this particular habitat.

Douglas Fir, Gray Oak, Birchleaf Buckthorn, and Mountain Mahogany are also common. Water flows along the canyon in the rainy season and during most winters.

Pine Canyon contains similar habitats but the Ponderosa Pine, Emory and Grave's oaks, Bigtooth Maple, Texas Madrone, and Mountain Sage are dominant, while Douglas Fir is rare and Arizona Cypress is completely absent. The rather extensive north-facing slope of the canyon contains a large stand of Ponderosa Pines. Pine Canyon has been established as a Natural Area in the International Biological Program. The area encompasses part of the pinyon-juniper woodlands along the lower drainage as well as the canyon bottom and the area of Ponderosa Pines. A similar environment also occurs in the Davis Mountains at Madera Canyon, which can be reached by automobile along Highway 118 west of Fort Davis.

This view from the Rio Grande Village Nature Trail includes the Rio Grande, Rio Grande Village Campground on the right bank, and the Chisos Mountains in the background.

Bird Finding

Finding a maximum number of birds can usually be accomplished by visiting all the different habitats within the various plant communities. If one wishes to find particular species of birds, however, it is most profitable to search only within suitable habitats at the proper time of year. One would be extremely unlikely to find a Painted Bunting at Boot Springs in December or a Townsend's Solitaire at Rio Grande Village in July.

There are several places within the park that a birder should visit if he is interested in a maximum number of species. Rio Grande Village is the best place I know for consistently finding a large number of birds. The major areas to search at Rio Grande Village include the cottonwood groves behind the store and to the west, the silt pond and the fish ponds next to the campground, the campground proper and the mesquite thickets just across the roadway to the north, the Rio Grande Village Nature Trail, and the adjacent desert hillsides.

The second most productive area is the Chisos Basin. This includes the drainage below the campground, the vicinity of the sewage lagoons, and the area along the Window Trail. I have made regular visits to the Basin Campground and the upper four-fifths of the Window Trail, returning along the trail to where one can follow the Oak Creek drainage upward past the sewage lagoons and to a point directly below the lower loop of the campground. From there one can return to the campground via a surfaced roadway.

There are several other localities within the park where approximately the same bird species can be found. Green Gulch can sometimes be quite productive, particularly during the fall migration. Upper Blue Creek Canyon is best in spring. Lower Pine Canyon can be a good area for bird watching except in midsummer.

In summer, a visit to Boot Canyon is a must. Although the Colima Warbler can usually be found at Laguna Meadow, the area between Boot Springs and the South Rim can be very productive. One of the best localities for consistently finding a good variety of birds, including the Colima Warbler from April 15 to September 1, is about two hundred yards beyond the cabin, where the canyon opens up slightly just beyond the Juniper Canyon side trail. Birders who are not able to walk or ride horseback to Boot Springs can usually find most of the same birds at Laguna Meadow. Laguna Meadow is one mile closer (three and one-half miles) to the Chisos Basin. Another area that can be very good in spring, summer, and fall is the Lost Mine Trail. This trail starts at 5,800 feet elevation and a two-mile walk offers some high-country exposure for the minimum of time. The Lost Mine Trail, however, is never as productive, birdwise, as are Boot Canyon and Laguna Meadow.

In late fall and early winter one can hardly go wrong in a visit to Castolon. The weedy fields adjacent to the roadway to Santa Elena, Mexico, and along Alamo Creek can produce more sparrows than anywhere else in the park. Dugout Wells, located just below Panther Junction on the road to Rio Grande Village, can be very productive during the spring migration.

For those birders who like to find a bench and sit and wait

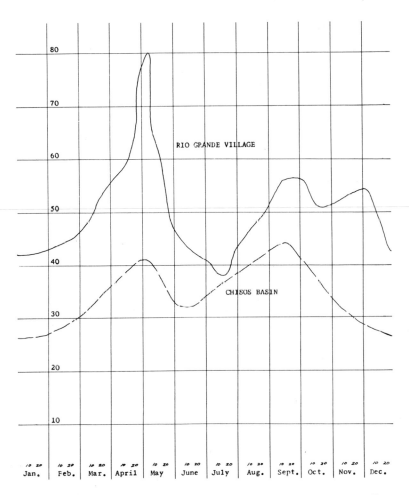

Figure 1. Seasonal variation of bird species averaged over a five-year period

for what feathered friends happen by, two places are suggested: the Old Ranch and the Rio Grande Village Nature Trail. The nature trail already has been discussed. The Old Ranch is located along the Castolon Road and is situated on Cottonwood Creek. Although the creek is dry most of the year, birds gather at the Old Ranch because of the water available from a working windmill. A bench, located beneath the walnuts and willows, is a relaxing place to bird with the minimum of effort.

Less than 10 percent of Big Bend's avifauna is considered to be permanent resident. The majority spend only a few hours to a few months within the area as migrants, or as summering or wintering residents. As a result, Big Bend's avian composition and density fluctuate considerably. The seasonal variation of bird species at Rio Grande Village (1,900 feet elevation) and the Chisos Basin (5,400 feet elevation) are illustrated in Figure 1. This is based upon field trips of three to five hours' duration throughout the year from August 1, 1966, to June 30, 1971. A total of 293 field trips were made to Rio Grande Village, and 109 to the Chisos Basin. The graph's high points represent periods of migration, which result in a great surge of birds through the area in spring, but only a moderate increase in fall. The low points illustrate the periods of minimal bird numbers: June 5 to 20 for the Chisos Basin, and July 10 to 20 for Rio Grande Village. The earlier increase in mountain species can be attributed to the post-nesting movement of lowland nesters away from the breeding grounds into the mountains.

THE MIGRATION

Spring may arrive early in the Big Bend. The first sign of the spring migration usually occurs before the end of February with the arrival of Violet-green Swallows along the Rio Grande. Black Dalea and Black Brush Acacia begin to bloom in lowland washes by early March, and their aromatic flowers may attract Lucifer and Black-chinned hummingbirds. By mid-March, spring migration is evident throughout the desert. Numbers of spring migrants increase gradually throughout late March, accelerate rapidly in April, and reach a peak during the last days of April and the first week of May. The high point is followed by a rather swift decrease in the number of species that are passing through the area during the rest of May and early June.

Northbound migrants are far more numerous within the lowlands, particularly along the river, than in the mountains. This great difference in numbers of species that can be found at Rio Grande Village and at the Chisos Basin is readily apparent in Figure 1, in spite of the highs for both localities falling within the same period. The maximum numbers of birds that I have recorded at these two localities are fifty-two species at the Basin within five hours on April 27, 1969, and ninety-three species at Rio Grande Village within six hours on May 3, 1970.

As an example of what birds can be found at this maximum period, the list of ninety-three species recorded at Rio Grande Village included the Least and Pied-billed grebes, American Bittern, Gadwall, Green-winged and Blue-winged teals, American Widgeon, Shoveler, Turkey and Black vultures, the Sharpshinned, Redtail, and Sparrow hawks, Common Gallinule, American Coot, Killdeer, Spotted and Solitary sandpipers, the White-winged, Mourning, Ground, and Inca doves, Yellow-billed Cuckoo, Roadrunner, Groove-billed Ani, Great Horned Owl, Lesser Nighthawk, White-throated Swift, Black-chinned Hummingbird, Ladder-backed Woodpecker, Western Kingbird, the Ash throated, Olive-sided, and Vermilion flycatchers, Say's Phoebe, Western Wood Pewee, the Violet-green, Rough-winged, Barn, and Cliff swallows, Common Raven, Verdin, House and Long-billed Marsh wrens, Mockingbird, Curve-billed Thrasher, Hermit Thrush, Black-tailed Gnatcatcher, Ruby-crowned Kinglet, Water Pipit, Cedar Waxwing, the Bell's, Solitary, and Warbling vireos, the Lucy's, Parula, Yellow, Audubon's, Townsend's, McGillivray's, Hooded, and Wilson's warblers, Northern Waterthrush, Yellowthroat, Yellow-breasted Chat, American Redstart, House Sparrow, Brewer's Blackbird, the Orchard, Hooded, Scott's, and Black-vented

orioles, Brown-headed Cowbird, Western and Summer tanagers, Cardinal, Pyrrhuloxia, Blue Grosbeak, Indigo and Painted
buntings, Dickcissel, House Finch, Lesser Goldfinch, Green-
tailed and Brown towhees, and the Lark, Black-throated, Chipping, Clay-colored, Brewer's, White-crowned, Lincoln's, and
Swamp sparrows.

Many of the birds found at Rio Grande Village were also
recorded in the Basin on April 27, 1969. Those species that were
recorded only in the Basin included the Scaled Quail, Blue-
throated Hummingbird, Acorn Woodpecker, the Hammond's,
Dusky, and Gray flycatchers, Mexican Jay, Black-crested Titmouse, Bushtit, the Bewick's, Cactus, Cañon, and Rock wrens,
Blue-gray Gnatcatcher, Gray Vireo, Pine Siskin, Rufous-sided
Towhee, Gray-headed Junco, and Rufous-crowned and Black-
chinned sparrows.

Fall migration in the lowlands is only a shadow of the spring
movement. Although post-nesting herons and shorebirds may
reach the river area in mid-July, the majority of the southbound birds do not begin to increase until the last of the month.
A gradual build-up continues throughout August, reaches a
peak in mid-September, and drops off during October. There is
a second but lighter increase during late November and the
first few days of December.

Mountain birds begin to increase immediately after the
northward movement subsides. Some post-nesting floodplain
and desert birds move to the mountains in June. The first of
the southbound migrants is the Rufous Hummingbird. It may
reach the mountain slopes by late August, and a peak is reached
in mid-September. This high point is followed by a gradual but
steady decrease in migrants. Movement through the mountains
is heavier in fall than in spring, although it is still considerably
less than along the Rio Grande.

The differences in spring and fall movements of birds
through the park area may be explained two ways. First, the
period of the northbound migration is shorter. It has a rather
moderate build-up but drops off swiftly. Conversely, the southward movement is more gradual and is scattered out over three

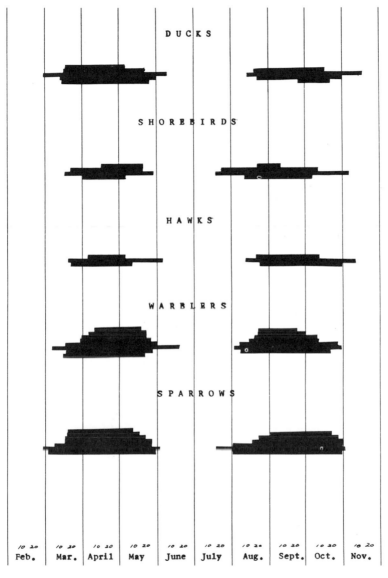

Figure 2. Relative abundance of five groups of migratory birds

and one-half months compared to only two months in spring. Second, the number of birds that pass through the park is less in fall than in spring. This is due at least partly to the topography of the Big Bend Country. Spring migrants follow north-south desert valleys and are naturally funneled into the lower Big Bend along the western edge of the Sierra del Carmens that form the eastern edge of the park and run south into Mexico for almost one hundred miles. Fall migrants are often diverted toward the southeast by the Santiago Mountains that form a barrier to lowland migrants just north of the park. I have watched flocks of blackbirds and individual gulls and hawks change their southward course toward the southeast, the Black Gap Refuge and the eastern side of the Sierra del Carmens, as they approach the ridges just north of Persimmon Gap.

Figure 2 illustrates the relative abundance of five groups of birds that are regular migrants through the Big Bend Country. Ducks begin to move through the area during the last of February and in early March. They become common along the river and at adjacent ponds from mid-March through May 20, and stragglers continue to pass through the area until mid-June. Fall migrants are less numerous; post-nesting birds may reach the Big Bend during the second week of August, but the peak of the fall movement does not occur until late September and lasts through October. Southbound birds continue to pass through the area in small numbers until early November, and stragglers can usually be found along the river until late November. During very mild winters the fall migration may be only one-half as great as that of normal years. Late winters may result in a movement of waterfowl through the park as much as three to five weeks later.

Shorebirds are never common within the Big Bend. In spite of the fact that the Rio Grande is a logical pathway for migrating waterbirds, only twenty kinds of shorebirds have been recorded within the park. These birds do not reach the area until mid-March in spring. They become most numerous from mid-April to early May, decrease considerably to mid-May, and stragglers continue to move through the area until the end of the month. The Killdeer is the park's only nesting shorebird. Fall migrants reach the Big Bend quite early; Spotted, Solitary. Baird's, and Least sandpipers may appear by mid-July. The total southward movement extends from mid-July through early November, with a minor peak evident from August 20 to September 12.

Migrant hawks are rather sporadic within the Big Bend. They usually are found alone or in twos or threes; there are no waves of hawks like those characteristic to the eastern part of the country. Early spring migrants reach the park in mid-March, a peak is reached during the last three weeks of April and early May, and stragglers continue to pass through the Big Bend until the first of June. Fall migrants begin to appear in mid-August, reach a high from late August to mid-October. and decline in numbers through the rest of the month. Migrant hawks can usually be found until about November 12.

The movement of warblers through the Big Bend produces the largest numbers of birds representative to any single family. Some spring migrants can be found during the second week of March, and the number of northbound migrants increases greatly during the last of the month and early April. The peak is reached during the last of April and the first half of May, but migrants remain fairly numerous within the Big Bend until May 25, and stragglers can usually be found throughout the first half of June. Southbound Black-and-white Warblers have been recorded as early as July 18, but most of the early fall migrants do not reach the Big Bend until early August. These early birds have been found within the mountains only; lowland migrants do not begin until mid-August. The fall movement is not as dramatic as that in the spring, and a population peak is reached from late August through September 20. Southbound birds can usually be found throughout October, although only two or three species are usually all that are found by the last of the month.

The sparrow migration is rather sporadic within the Big Bend, and is generally restricted to the lowlands below 5,000 feet elevation. Some movement is evident during the last days

of February, but the main spring migration does not get underway until mid-March. Sparrows continue to be common migrants throughout April and until late May. Stragglers can
usually be found within the Big Bend until early June. Southbound Lark and Chipping sparrows may reach the park as
early as the last half of July, and Lark Buntings usually appear
during the first days of August. The bulk of the southbound
sparrow migration does not become regular until September
and lasts through October. Fall migrants continue to move
through the area until late November.

THE BREEDING SEASON

More than one hundred species of birds have been found to
nest within Big Bend National Park in recent years. Lowland
residents are first to begin their territorial defense and to nest.
Some of the desert species may be incubating before the first of
April, and some mountain birds may not arrive on their breeding grounds until late April.

Nesting birds of the *floodplain* include a few permanent
residents, but the majority reside within the Big Bend only
during the spring and summer months. Most of these arrive in
late March and April. The last of the summer residents to
reach the area are the Yellow-billed Cuckoo and the Blue Grosbeak. The most conspicuous breeding birds of the floodplain
include the Mourning and White-winged doves, Black-chinned
Hummingbird, Bell's Vireo, Yellow-breasted Chat, Brown-
headed Cowbird, Summer Tanager, Painted Bunting, Cardinal,
and Blue Grosbeak. Other species that are regular nesters within the floodplain habitat are the Yellow-billed Cuckoo, Roadrunner, Screech and Elf owls, Ladder-backed Woodpecker,
Black Phoebe, Ash-throated Flycatcher, Verdin, Mockingbird,
Black-tailed Gnatcatcher, Orchard and Hooded orioles, Pyrrhuloxia, and House Finch.

The Rio Grande Village Nature Trail offers an accessible
floodplain habitat where all the above species can usually be
observed with a little searching. Typical floodplain areas exist
at a number of other localities including Hot Springs, San

Birds of the Floodplain. (*Left column, top to bottom*) Yellow-billed Cuckoo, *Coccyzus americanus*; Summer Tanager, *Piranga rubra*; Bell's Vireo, *Vireo bellii*; Yellowthroat, *Geothlypis trichas*; Cardinal, *Richmondena cardinalis*. (*Right column, top to bottom*) White-winged Dove, *Zenaida asiatica*; Cliff Swallow, *Petrochelidon pyrrhonota*; Yellow-breasted Chat, *Icteria virens*; Painted Bunting, *Passerina ciris*; Black Phoebe, *Sayornis nigricans*.

Vicente Crossing, and the Santa Elena Canyon picnic area. If sufficient water is present to form ponds or marshy areas, as at Rio Grande Village, the Pied-billed Grebe, Sora, American Coot, Killdeer, and Yellowthroat may find suitable nesting sites.

The *arroyos* offer a drier environment where many of the same birds often can be found nesting. The most conspicuous breeding birds of this community include the Verdin, Cactus Wren, Mockingbird, Black-tailed Gnatcatcher, Pyrrhuloxia, and House Finch. The Scaled Quail and Lesser Nighthawk are ground-nesters that find suitable conditions for nesting under the shrubby thickets of mesquite and acacia, and the larger shrubs may offer suitable holes for the nesting Screech and Elf owls, Ladder-backed Woodpecker, and Ash-throated Fly-catcher.

Dugout Wells, Glenn Springs, Panther Junction, and the Old Ranch are examples of arroyo vegetation that result from water-catching places in the upper arroyos. These localities offer suitable nesting habitats for the White-winged and Mourning doves, Yellow-billed Cuckoo, Bell's Vireo, Yellow-breasted Chat, Summer Tanager, Blue Grosbeak, Painted Bunting, Lesser Goldfinch, and House Finch.

The *shrub desert* is the largest of Big Bend's plant communities but offers the least appealing environment to breeding birds. Of most importance are the rocky ledges and cliffs that may occur from the edge of the Rio Grande to the lower canyons of the mountains. This habitat is utilized by the Turkey and Black vultures, Red-tailed, Zone-tailed, and Sparrow hawks, Peregrine and Prairie falcons, Golden Eagle, Great Horned Owl, White-throated Swift, Say's Phoebe, Cliff Swallow, Common Raven, and Cañon and Rock wrens. The Cliff Swallow also nests under concrete bridges, such as those over Tornillo and Alamo creeks.

The plants of the open desert support few breeding birds; the majority of the perching birds seen within this environment nest within adjacent arroyos. Nesting birds of the shrub desert include the Scaled Quail, Roadrunner, Ash-throated Fly-

Birds of the Arroyos and the Shrub Desert. (*Left column, top to bottom*)
Ash-throated Flycatcher, *Myiarchus cinerascens*; Lesser Nighthawk, *Chordeiles acutipennis*; Black-tailed Gnatcatcher, *Polioptila melanura*; Verdin, *Auriparus flaviceps*, at nest; Scaled Quail, *Callipepla squamata*. (*Right column, top to bottom*) Mockingbird, *Mimus polyglottos*; Black-throated Sparrow, *Amphispiza bilineata*; Cactus Wren, *Campylorhynchus brunneicapillus*; Roadrunner, *Geococcyx californianus*.

Birds of the Grassland. (*Left column, top to bottom*) Pyrrhuloxia, *Pyrrhuloxia sinuata*; Loggerhead Shrike, *Lanius ludovicianus*; Brown Towhee, *Pipilo fuscus*; Elf Owl, *Micrathene whitneyi*. (*Right column, top to bottom*) Scott's Oriole, *Icterus parisorum*; Ladder-backed Woodpecker, *Dendrocopos scalaris*; Varied Bunting, *Passerina versicolor*; Black-chinned Sparrow, *Spizella atrogularis*; Rufous-crowned Sparrow, *Aimophila ruficeps*.

catcher, Pyrrhuloxia, House Finch, and Black-throated Sparrow. The Black-throated Sparrow is the only species that is more common within this community than any other.

The *grasslands* may be considered the transition zone between the desert and arroyos and the mountain woodlands. Therefore, a large number of birds from both of the adjacent communities utilize the grasslands. Yet in spite of this overlap, there are several species unique to the area. Conspicuous grassland birds include the Loggerhead Shrike, Scott's Oriole, Pyrrhuloxia, Blue Grosbeak, Varied Bunting, Brown Towhee, and the Rufous-crowned, Cassin's, and Black-chinned sparrows. Other regular breeding species of the grasslands include the Scaled Quail, Roadrunner, Elf Owl, Poor-will, Ladderbacked Woodpecker, Ash-throated Flycatcher, Verdin, Cactus Wren, Mockingbird, Black-tailed Gnatcatcher, Brown-headed Cowbird, House Finch, and Black-throated Sparrow.

Some of the better localities in which to find grassland birds include the vicinity of Panther Junction, lower Pine Canyon, Green Gulch, and along the central section of the Window Trail. Because of the combined habitats of grasslands and deciduous woodlands along the Window Trail, this can be one of the better localities for finding a large assortment of birds during summer. A typical list of birds to be seen there is one recorded during the morning of May 25, 1968. It included the Turkey Vulture, Sparrow Hawk, Scaled Quail, White-winged and Mourning doves, White-throated Swift, Black-chinned and Blue-throated hummingbirds, Acorn Woodpecker, Ash-throated Flycatcher, Say's Phoebe, Violet-green Swallow, Mexican Jay, Common Raven, Black-crested Titmouse, Bushtit, the Cactus, Cañon, and Rock wrens, Mockingbird, Crissal Thrasher, Blue-gray Gnatcatcher, Gray Vireo, Scott's Oriole, Brown-headed Cowbird, Hepatic and Summer tanagers, Black-headed and Blue grosbeaks, Varied Bunting, House Finch, Lesser Goldfinch, Brown Towhee, and Rufous-crowned Sparrow.

The *pinyon-juniper-oak woodlands* consist of a variety of habitats that may be divided into two different plant associations, the deciduous and the pinyon-juniper woodlands. For the

Birds of the Pinyon-Juniper-Oak Woodlands. (*Left column, top to bottom*) Mexican Jay, *Aphelocoma ultramarina*; Hepatic Tanager, *Piranga flava*; Blue-gray Gnatcatcher, *Polioptila caerulea*; Cañon Wren, *Catherpes mexicanus*; Bewick's Wren, *Thryomanes bewickii*. (*Right column, top to bottom*) Acorn Woodpecker, *Melanerpes formicivorus*; Black-crested Titmouse, *Parus atricristatus*; Bushtit, *Psaltriparus minimus* (black-eared phase on left); Rufous-sided Towhee, *Pipilo erythrophthalmus*.

Birds of the Cypress-Pine-Oak Woodlands. (*Left column, top to bottom*) Black-headed Grosbeak, *Pheucticus melanocephalus*; Hutton's Vireo, *Vireo huttoni*; Western Flycatcher, *Empidonax difficilis*; Colima Warbler, *Vermivora crissalis*; Whip-poor-will, *Caprimulgus vociferus*. (*Right column, top to bottom*) Band-tailed Pigeon, *Columba fasciata*; Red-shafted Flicker, *Colaptes cafer*; White-breasted Nuthatch, *Sitta carolinensis*; Flammulated Owl, *Otus flammeolus*.

Wintering Birds. (*Left column, top to bottom*) Orange-crowned Warbler, *Vermivora celata*; Myrtle Warbler, *Dendroica coronata*; Eastern Phoebe, *Sayornis phoebe*; House Finch, *Carpodacus mexicanus*; White-crowned Sparrow, *Zonotrichia leucophrys*; Green-winged Teal, *Anas carolinensis*. (*Right column, top to bottom*) Audubon's Warbler, *Dendroica auduboni*; Ruby-crowned Kinglet, *Regulus calendula*; Vermilion Flycatcher, *Pyrocephalus rubinus*; Yellow-bellied Sapsucker, *Sphyrapicus varius*; Swamp Sparrow, *Melospiza georgiana*.

most part, these zones of vegetation are interspersed and may be regarded as a single unit. Although a nesting bird may prefer a broadleaf tree over a conifer, it is likely that its total territory includes both. Therefore, the breeding avifauna will be regarded as one.

Typical breeding birds of this woodland community within the Chisos Mountains include the Screech Owl, Broad-tailed Hummingbird, Acorn Woodpecker, Ash-throated Flycatcher, Mexican Jay, Black-crested Titmouse, Bushtit, Bewick's and Cañon wrens, Blue-gray Gnatcatcher, Hepatic Tanager, Black-headed Grosbeak, Rufous-sided and Brown towhees, and Rufous-crowned Sparrow. Several species nest within the lower parts of this community and rarely, if ever, breed above 5,500 feet elevation. Those species include the White-winged and Mourning doves, Great Horned and Elf owls, Black-chinned Hummingbird, Ladder-backed Woodpecker, Gray Vireo, Brown-headed Cowbird, Scott's Oriole, Summer Tanager, and House Finch. Those that rarely occur in the lower parts of the pinyon-juniper-oak woodlands but are fairly common nesters in the highlands include the Zone-tailed Hawk, Whip-poor-will, White-breasted Nuthatch, and Hutton's Vireo.

Laguna Meadow is an excellent place to find typical breeding birds of the pinyon-juniper-oak community. A two-hour visit there, on the morning of June 6, 1968, resulted in the recording of the Turkey Vulture, Red-tailed and Sparrow hawks, Band-tailed Pigeon, White-throated Swift, Acorn and Ladder-backed woodpeckers, Ash-throated Flycatcher, Mexican Jay, Black-crested Titmouse, Bushtit, White-breasted Nuthatch. Bewick's Wren, Crissal Thrasher, Blue-gray Gnatcatcher, Hutton's Vireo, Black-headed Grosbeak, House Finch. Lesser Goldfinch, Rufous-sided and Brown towhees, and Rufous-crowned and Black-chinned sparrows.

The *cypress-pine-oak woodlands* are restricted to only a few localities within the Chisos Mountains. Boot Canyon contains the best example of this community, but Pine Canyon offers all the same birds in summer, with the exception of the Colima

Warbler. The most conspicuous breeding birds to be found in Boot Canyon are the Band-tailed Pigeon, Broad-tailed and Blue-throated hummingbirds, Red-shafted Flicker, Acorn Woodpecker, Western Flycatcher, Mexican Jay, Black-crested Titmouse, Cañon Wren, Hutton's Vireo, Colima Warbler, Blackheaded Grosbeak, and Rufous-sided Towhee. Less conspicuous but regular nesting birds of this woodland community are the Sharp-shinned Hawk, Flammulated Owl, Whip-poor-will, Bushtit, White-breasted Nuthatch, Bewick's Wren, and Rufous-crowned Sparrow.

THE WINTER MONTHS

It is reasonably safe to consider the period from mid-November to late February as wintertime within the Big Bend Country. During fall periods that are warmer than normal, however, some southward movement may be detected until mid-December. Conversely, during fall periods that are colder than normal, the majority of the southbound migrants may already be south of the border by early November.

Wintering bird populations vary considerably from wet years to dry ones. Sparrows are common in winter following summer and fall periods of above-average precipitation but usually are rare following a dry summer and fall. A few groups of birds and individual species are sporadic in occurrence. Waterfowl, hawks, and a number of northern species, such as the Williamson's Sapsucker, Red-breasted and Pygmy nuthatches, Brown Creeper, Cassin's Finch, and Red Crossbill, may be present during some winters and completely absent others. During warmer winters, the Ash-throated and Dusky flycatchers, Blue-gray Gnatcatcher, and Bewick's Wren are more numerous than in colder winters.

The best possible index to wintering birds is the Christmas Bird Counts. These counts are part of a national effort, sponsored by the National Audubon Society and the United States Fish and Wildlife Service, of censusing areas to determine bird populations on one day during the last two weeks of each year. The counts indicate bird movement, increases and decreases of populations, and locations of wintering populations. Three different counts have been taken in Big Bend National Park in recent years. Only two counts were taken in 1966— at Rio Grande Village and the Chisos Mountains—but three areas were surveyed in 1967, 1968, 1969, and 1970; the Castolon–Santa Elena Canyon vicinity represents the third count area. Fourteen Christmas Counts have been taken over the five years. The Rio Grande Village counts were highest each year; a maximum of eighty-five species was recorded in 1968. Rio Grande Village is undoubtedly the best birding area, throughout the year, within Big Bend National Park.

One hundred forty-seven species of birds were recorded on the fourteen Christmas Counts. Only nineteen species were recorded on all fourteen counts. Those individuals, which may be considered the most common of the park's wintering birds, include the Sparrow Hawk, Scaled Quail, Ladder-backed Woodpecker, Say's Phoebe, Common Raven, Verdin, Bewick's, Cactus, Cañon, and Rock wrens, Mockingbird, Hermit Thrush, Ruby-crowned Kinglet, Loggerhead Shrike, Orange-crowned Warbler, Pyrrhuloxia, House Finch, Green-tailed Towhee, and White-crowned Sparrow.

A total of six species was recorded on thirteen of the Christmas Counts: the Red-tailed Hawk, Mourning Dove, Red shafted Flicker, Yellow-bellied Sapsucker, House Wren, and Rufoussided Towhee. The Roadrunner, and House and Chipping sparrows were seen on twelve counts. The Cooper's Hawk, Blacktailed Gnatcatcher, Meadowlark, Cardinal, and Cassin's, Black-throated, and Lincoln's sparrows were recorded eleven times. Twelve species were seen on ten counts: the Sharpshinned Hawk, White-winged Dove, Black Phoebe, Curvebilled and Crissal thrashers, Myrtle and Audubon's warblers, Lesser Goldfinch, Brown Towhee, and Brewer's, Swamp, and Song sparrows.

Eight kinds of birds were recorded on nine of the Christmas Counts: the Spotted Sandpiper, Eastern Phoebe, Rough-winged Swallow, Robin, Slate-colored Junco, and Savannah, Vesper, and Rufous-crowned sparrows. The Killdeer, Screech and Great

Horned owls, Ash-throated Flycatcher, Long-billed Marsh Wren, Sage Thrasher, Blue-gray Gnatcatcher, Water Pipit, Cedar Waxwing, Yellowthroat, and Lark Bunting were found on eight counts. The Great Blue Heron, Common Snipe, Eastern Bluebird, Gray-headed Junco, and Field and White-throated sparrows were counted seven times. Seven species were found on six counts: the Green-winged Teal, Black Vulture, Marsh Hawk, American Coot, Dusky Flycatcher, Golden-crowned Kinglet, and Oregon Junco. The Yellow-shafted Flicker, Acorn Woodpecker, Vermilion Flycatcher, Mexican Jay, Black-crested Titmouse, Bushtit, Townsend's Solitaire, Pine Siskin, and Black-chinned Sparrow were recorded on five counts. Nine species were recorded four times: the Golden Eagle, Sora, Least Sandpiper, White-throated Swift, Brown Thrasher, Phainopepla, Hutton's Vireo, Townsend's Warbler, and Grasshopper Sparrow.

Eight species were counted on three counts: the Ring-necked Duck, Ground Dove, Belted Kingfisher, White-breasted Nuthatch, Brown Creeper, Carolina Wren, Western Bluebird, and Great-tailed Grackle. Eleven kinds of birds were found on two of the Christmas Counts: the Gadwall, Pintail, Canvasback, Ferruginous Hawk, Band-tailed Pigeon, Anna's Hummingbird. Williamson's Sapsucker, Winter Wren, Scott's Oriole, Rusty Blackbird, and Cassin's Finch. And twenty-nine species were recorded on only one of the counts: the Eared and Least grebes. Green Heron, Whistling Swan, Mallard, Blue-winged Teal. American Widgeon, Shoveler, Wood Duck, Bufflehead, Harris' Hawk, Prairie Falcon, Western Sandpiper, Long-eared Owl. Broad-tailed and Rufous hummingbirds, Thick-billed Kingbird. Horned Lark, Scrub Jay, Red-breasted Nuthatch, Mountain Bluebird, Starling, Gray Vireo, Parula Warbler, Brewer's Blackbird, Varied Bunting, and Baird's, Lark, and Fox sparrows.

Annotated List of Species

The following is an annotated list of 385 species of birds that have been reported for Big Bend National Park and vicinity. The majority of these—359—are included in the regular list of species, but 26 are regarded as hypothetical and are included in a second list, "Birds of Uncertain Occurrence," which starts on page 205. Common and scientific names used are those given in the American Ornithologists' Union *Check-list of North American Birds*, fifth edition (1957), except for a few individuals that have since been proved to be incorrectly defined.

Several terms are used to describe the status of the various birds within the area. The terms *abundant, common, fairly common, uncommon,* and *rare* are used and are defined as follows:

Abundant—Birds that can be found in numbers, without any particular search, in the proper habitat at the right time of year.

Common—Birds that can almost always be found, in smaller numbers and with a minimum of searching, in the proper habitat at the right time of year.

Fairly common—Birds that can sometimes be found, in small numbers and with some searching, in the proper habitat at the right time of year.

Uncommon—Birds that are seldom seen, and usually in small numbers or alone, in the proper habitat at the right time of year.

Rare—Birds that are encountered only by chance; those out of normal range and always a surprise.

A few other terms used that need to be clarified are as follows:

Permanent resident—Birds that remain within the area throughout the year; they do not migrate.

Summer resident—Birds that breed within the area; they may arrive as early as March and remain as late as October.

Post-nesting visitor—Birds that visit the area in summer but do not breed there; those that wander to the Big Bend after nesting.

Migrant—Birds that pass through the area only in spring and/or fall from March to May and August to November.

Winter resident—Birds that remain within the area during winter; they may arrive as early as September and remain as late as April.

LOONS: Family Gaviidae

COMMON LOON. *Gavia immer*

The only record for the park is a bird collected on the river near Solis by A. G. Clark on October 17, 1937 (Borell. 1938). Since this species prefers larger bodies of water than those found within the park, it is a vagrant only. Common Loons, however, as well as the Arctic (*Gavia arctica*) and Red-throated (*Gavia stellata*) loons, have been seen on Lake Balmorhea (thirty-five miles north of the Davis Mountains) during winter months in recent years.

GREBES: Family Podicipedidae

EARED GREBE. *Podiceps caspicus*

Uncommon migrant and rare winter visitor on the Rio

Grande and adjacent ponds. It has been seen most often in the vicinity of Rio Grande Village from October 26 through December; the only spring sighting is one by Brodrick at Rio Grande Village in March, 1963.

LEAST GREBE. *Podiceps dominicus*

As far as can be determined, only one or two birds have been seen within the Big Bend area. A lone individual arrived August 5, 1969, and remained until early July, 1970. It was seen by numerous birders and photographed by Ty Hotchkiss. On April 15, 1971, I found a lone bird on the Rio Grande Village silt pond, where the first bird had last been seen. The Least Grebe had previously been recorded in the United States only in the lower Rio Grande Valley of southern Texas and north to Bexar County, and in southern Arizona and California.

PIED-BILLED GREBE. *Podilymbus podiceps*

Rare summer and winter resident and fairly common migrant. It probably would be more numerous during the breeding season if it were not for the scarcity of suitable water areas throughout most of the Big Bend Country. Even at suitable habitats, such as the cattail-filled silt pond at Rio Grande Village, it does not nest every year. Siglin observed an adult with young on its back there on July 28, 1967, and I found four free-swimming, fledged young on August 1. On May 17, 1970, I again heard and observed two birds courting at the same pond. They remained there throughout the summer and assumedly nested. It is of interest that the birds nested there only in 1967 and 1970, the only two years that the silt pond was dredged. None nested there during the intervening years. Perhaps their nesting requirements exclude a pond without an adjacent deep pond or a running channel.

Pied-billed Grebes are most often seen on open, quiet stretches of the river and on adjacent ponds during migration from early March through May and September 1 to November 23. There are no December sightings in the park, but it has been recorded at Rio Grande Village a number of times in January and February.

PELICANS: Family Pelecanidae
WHITE PELICAN. *Pelecanus erythrorhynchos*

There are but three records of this species for the Big Bend. The Hoffmans first reported it from near Santa Elena Canyon, May 18 to 24, 1957. On April 1, 1963, Park Ranger Lloyd Whitt acquired a bird band taken from a "large white bird" found dead in the Rio Grande near Castolon by a Mexican boy who had carried the band in his pocket for more than a year. Fish and Wildlife Service banding records showed it to be from a White Pelican banded at Gunnison Island on the Great Salt Lake in Utah, June 19, 1947. J. A. Roosevelt also found a White Pelican at Roosevelt Lake, in western Jeff Davis County, in April, 1956. A Brown Pelican (*Pelecanus occidentalis*) was reported from this same location by Roosevelt in October, 1955 (Pansy Espy).

CORMORANTS: Family Phalacrocoracidae
OLIVACEOUS CORMORANT. *Phalacrocorax olivaceus*

This little cormorant has been reported for the Big Bend Country only twice. Thompson G. Marsh observed two along Terlingua Creek, at the mouth of Santa Elena Canyon, on March 23, 1960, and described them as being the "size of mergansers." Twenty-two days later, on April 14, Brodrick found a lone Olivaceous Cormorant on the river at Solis, more than forty miles below Santa Elena Canyon.

HERONS and BITTERNS: Family Ardaidae
GREAT BLUE HERON. *Ardea herodias*

Rare in summer but a fairly common migrant and winter visitor. This large, graceful bird appears to be present along the Rio Grande all year. There are no records of nesting, although Sutton and Semple did observe an adult and an "immature" bird near Boquillas on May 21, 1935. It is likely that this species once nested along the river, but today, between Boquillas and Presidio, there is only a single grove of cottonwoods and willows large enough to support a rookery; it is located on the floodplain near Santa Elena Crossing, where there probably is too much human activity for nesting herons.

There is an increase in sightings during late September, and migrants are most common from mid-October to early November and from early March through the first week of May. Wintering birds can be expected anywhere along the river and at adjacent ponds.

GREEN HERON. *Butorides virescens*

Uncommon in summer, fairly common in migration. There is one series of winter sightings at Rio Grande Village from December 22, 1970, through January 31, 1971 (Wauer). Most park records of this little heron range from April 1 through November 19. Although there are no recent records of nesting, it is present along the river during May and June, and nesting is likely at appropriate places along the floodplain. Van Tyne and Sutton discovered a nest, containing four eggs, twelve feet high in a mesquite near the river at Castolon on May 7, 1935. The breeding race was identified as the western form, *anthonyi*. Palmer (1962) reported that the eastern race is known to nest eastward from Pecos and Fort Stockton, Texas.

The spring migration is heavier than that in fall, and the northern movement reaches a peak from May 1 to 19. Postnesting wanderers and early fall migrants may appear by mid-August. Except for a two-week peak in early September, the fall migration seems to start early and drag along to mid-November. Most records are from the lowlands, but Pansy Espy reported this heron at 6,000 feet elevation at a stock tank near Pine Peak in the Davis Mountains on October 10, 1969.

LITTLE BLUE HERON. *Florida caerulea*

There is a single record of this little heron for the park. A lone bird was seen fishing along Tornillo Creek at Hot Springs by Mrs. Harreey Christensen on March 11, 1971. That same day, Mrs. Ward Woodrich observed the bird at this same location.

CATTLE EGRET. *Bubulcus ibis*

A migrant, reported for the Big Bend Country only since 1967. Roger Siglin and Gary Blyth first observed one at Rio Grande Village on October 27, 1967. I found one at Boquillas Crossing on April 7, 1968, and the Whitsons saw ten individuals at Rio Grande Village on April 22. Another loner was found along the desert roadside near Dugout Wells on September 14, 1968 (Wauer); Hershel Fowler, Paul Gerrish, and Sharon Wauer saw one at Panther Junction on October 23, 1969; one was seen at Rio Grande Village on a number of occasions from September 12 to 16, 1970; and Stoney Burdick and I found twenty-two there on October 29, 1971. According to Wolfe (1956), this exotic bird has been found in Texas only since 1955. It apparently is spreading quite rapidly throughout the state and can be expected to increase within the Big Bend Country, particularly in spring and fall. A specimen taken at Lake Balmorhea on October 21, 1969, is in the Sul Ross State University collection.

COMMON EGRET. *Casmerodius albus*

Uncommon migrant in spring. There are only two fall sightings, lone birds at Rio Grande Village on September 28, 1966, and September 18, 1970 (Wauer). This large, white bird is a regular spring migrant from April 8 to May 16, when it has been recorded singly or in twos and threes. There also are four records from June 10 to 17, which may represent post-nesting visitors. An August 1, 1968, sighting (Wauer) at Rio Grande Village is certainly a post-nesting wanderer.

SNOWY EGRET. *Leucophoyx thula*

Rare but regular spring migrant along the river from April 11 to May 7. There is a single fall record at Rio Grande Village on September 14, 1969 (Wauer).

LOUISIANA HERON. *Hydranassa tricolor*

Rare migrant and regular post-nesting visitor along the river and at adjacent ponds. Although there were no records of this beautiful bird before 1967, since then it has been seen on several occasions from April 5 to May 24 and August 1 to September 11. I have found it surprisingly unafraid at times; on several occasions I have walked to within a few yards of birds feeding along the shore of the larger pond at Rio Grande Village.

BLACK-CROWNED NIGHT HERON. *Nycticorax nycticorax*

Rare migrant, lone sightings in summer and winter. This species apparently has decreased in recent years. Van Tyne and Sutton reported it to be fairly common along the river in May, but there were only three park sightings during the 1960's; Sauvageau reported one at Rio Grande Village on January 17, 1966; the Davidsons found one there on April 13, 1967; and I saw one near Santa Elena Canyon on June 23, 1968. In 1971, one was found at Rio Grande Village on May 7 and 29 (Wauer).

YELLOW-CROWNED NIGHT HERON. *Nyctanassa violacea*

Rare migrant and regular post-nesting visitor along the river and adjacent ponds. It is strange that there were no reports of this nocturnal heron within the Big Bend area prior to 1967. I have found it a visitor to be expected at the ponds at Rio Grande Village after July 23. Fall migrants have been recorded as late as October 12; a specimen was taken there on September 13, 1967 (Wauer). The majority of these late summer and fall birds are juvenals. There is but one series of spring sightings—a lone bird at Rio Grande Village from April 26 to May 6, 1968 (Wauer and Whitsons).

LEAST BITTERN. *Ixorbrychus exilis*

Rare summer resident and migrant. There are no park records prior to 1966. A pair of Least Bitterns resided at the Rio Grande Village silt pond during June, 1967, and a pair was seen there on May 11, 1969, but I did not find a nest or see young birds. Other sightings, all at Rio Grande Village, include lone birds on April 20, 1967, and April 15, 1971 (Wauer), one observed by David and Roy Brown on April 27, 1966, one seen by the Peckhams and me on May 6, 1970, and one seen on September 9, 1967 (Wauer). This extremely shy bird may be more common in migration than records indicate.

AMERICAN BITTERN. *Botaurus lentiginosus*

Uncommon migrant from April 17 to May 20 in spring and from September 30 to November 10 in fall. There also is one earlier spring sighting, at Rio Grande Village on March 24, 1970 (Wauer). Although American Bitterns have been found regularly only along the Rio Grande to date, it should be looked for at stock tanks throughout the Big Bend Country during migration.

STORKS: Family Ciconiidae

WOOD STORK. *Mycteria americana*

There is a single record; Jerry Strickling observed one perched on a cottonwood tree at Dugout Wells on May 18, 1962. Since this species breeds along the Texas Gulf Coast and is known to wander after nesting, additional records in spring and late summer should be expected. This species is the "Wood Ibis" of earlier publications, but it is not an ibis.

IBISES and SPOONBILLS: Family Threskiornithidae

WHITE-FACED IBIS. *Plegadis chihi*

Rare migrant. Louis Greger was first to observe a lone bird

at Star Creek on Tornillo Flat in May, 1964. A flock of twenty birds was seen at Boquillas, during a dust storm, on January 25, 1965. I found eight birds at Rio Grande Village on September 11, 1970; a few remained until September 18. Pansy Espy recorded this species in the Davis Mountains on September 20, 1964, and Jody and Clay Miller reported it to be occasional at their ranch in western Jeff Davis County.

WHITE IBIS. *Eudocimus albus*

There is only one record of this tropical wader within Big Bend. The Joe Maxwells observed and photographed one along irrigation ditches at Rio Grande Village on February 6 or 7, 1971. It apparently was killed by a predator, because Philip F. Allan reported a dead White Ibis on February 8. The specimen was examined by Art Norton, who retained a number of feathers. I later obtained several characteristic primaries and deposited them in the Big Bend National Park study collection.

SWANS, GEESE, and DUCKS: Family Anatidae

WHISTLING SWAN. *Olor columbianus*

There are three records of this large, graceful bird in the Big Bend Country. William Lay Thompson (1953) reported twelve individuals at a stock tank at the Black Gap Wildlife Management Area, just north of the park, in December, 1951. All twelve of these birds were reportedly killed by local ranchers. Clay Miller found seven at his ranch on December 12, 1961, and Dick Youse observed three birds on the river at Rio Grande Village on December 30, 1969.

CANADA GOOSE. *Branta canadensis*

The only park record is that of a lone bird seen and heard calling as it flew over Rio Grande Village, November 30, 1967 (Wauer). It is not uncommon at Lake Balmorhea, however, and the Clay Millers have recorded this bird at their ranch in December and January in 1953, 1955, 1956, 1959, and 1960.

WHITE-FRONTED GOOSE. *Anser albifrons*

There is one record of this goose within the Big Bend area. Ty and Julie Hotchkiss saw it twice along the river at Rio Grande Village on April 29, 1969. They reported it to me the following day. After trying unsuccessfully to find the bird on May 1, I asked some of the Mexican boys at the Boquillas Crossing if any of them had seen a *pato grande* (large duck). Siverio Athayde said he had seen a large waterbird the previous day. Surprisingly enough, without hesitation he picked the White-fronted Goose from a series of ducks and geese shown him on three pages of *Birds of North America*.

SNOW GOOSE. *Chen hyperborea*

Rare winter visitor. The Bedells reported that a lone Snow Goose was seen several times at Rio Grande Village, along the river and at adjacent ponds, from March 6 to 21, 1963. On November 1, 1970, I observed a lone bird below Lajitas on the Mexican side of the Rio Grande. North of the park, Espy and the Millers have recorded it in Jeff Davis County on October 21 and November 21, 1958, on December 13, 1960, throughout the winter of 1961–62, and from February 11 to 28, 1970. Joe Robinette collected a specimen (Sul Ross collection) from a stock pond on the Wittenburg Ranch, Jeff Davis County, January 30, 1970, that was identified as a Ross' Goose (*Chen rossii*).

FULVOUS TREE DUCK. *Dendrocygna bicolor*

There is a single sighting of a lone bird found sitting on the Mexican bank of the river across from Rio Grande Village, April 18, 1967, by five capable birders whom I recorded only as Hanlon, McCarroll, Meyer, Kuehn, and Rowe. There is also a lone sighting in the Davis Mountains; Pansy Espy recorded one at the Caldwell Ranch in September, 1965.

MALLARD. *Anas platyrhynchos*

Uncommon fall migrant and winter visitor from October 9 through January. There also is a March 13, 1968, sighting of a lone female at Rio Grande Village (Wauer). One or two individuals usually spend December and January within the area, but Mallards cannot be expected regularly at a certain pond or stretch along the river. Apparently, this and most of the other wintering waterfowl wander along the river and visit ponds within the Big Bend Country and adjacent Mexico throughout their stay. Espy reports that this duck nests between Alpine and Fort Davis and north to Balmorhea.

MEXICAN DUCK. *Anas diazi*

Uncommon visitor along the Rio Grande and at Rio Grande Village. Most sightings are during spring, summer, and fall, but it is rare in winter as well. There is no indication that it nests within the park, but I have seen it on Calamity Creek (twenty miles south of Alpine on Highway 118) and north of Alpine along the Fort Davis Highway on a number of occasions during May and June. Ohlendorf and Patton (1971) observed an adult with six young sixteen miles southeast of Alpine on June 18, 1969, and Espy found "hatched young in an irrigation ditch between Toyahvale and Balmorhea." It apparently is a resident within the Big Bend and can be expected at water areas throughout. Most park records are of one or two birds, but Thompson Marsh observed five at Rio Grande Village on March 22, 1960.

BLACK DUCK. *Anas rubripes*

There is only one sighting of this eastern species within the park. On the morning of December 10, 1967, I found a lone Black Duck with a Mallard and Gadwall on a pond at Rio Grande Village; nearby was a Rusty Blackbird, another first sighting for the park. The previous day had been very stormy; snow had fallen on the nearby Carmen and Chisos mountains, and a strong southeastern wind had blown all day. Apparently these birds had arrived with the cold front.

GADWALL. *Anas strepera*

Fairly common migrant in spring, uncommon in fall, and uncommon in winter. It is most numerous along the river from mid-April through mid-May, but records range from August 23 through May 29. Although sightings of one to five individuals are most common, a flock of twenty was seen at Rio Grande Village on April 17, 1970 (Wauer).

PINTAIL. *Anas acuta*

Uncommon migrant and winter visitor in the park, can be abundant at Lake Balmorhea. Pintails have been recorded along the river from August 28 to March 22. Early fall arrivals may linger at ponds, such as those at Rio Grande Village, for several weeks before moving on. Most records are of one to four individuals, but I observed forty-three birds flying in a V-shaped formation over Rio Grande Village on February 13, 1968.

GREEN-WINGED TEAL. *Anas carolinensis*

Common migrant and winter visitor. This is Big Bend's most numerous waterfowl. It has been recorded from August 16 through May 18, mostly along the Rio Grande and at adjacent ponds. It also has been seen along Tornillo Creek, at Willow Tank and other tanks in the lowlands; five birds were seen on the sewage lagoons in the Chisos Basin on April 29, 1970 (Wauer).

BLUE-WINGED TEAL. *Anas discors*

Rare in summer and winter and common in migration. Summer sightings are few and far between, but apparently a few individuals remain throughout; I have recorded lone birds at Rio Grande Village on June 18, 1967, and July 17, 1968, and a pair on August 13, 1968. Blue-wings are most numerous along the river from early March through June 1, and again from August 27 through October. There is one mountain sighting; Ron Knaus observed a pair on the sewage lagoons in the Chisos Basin May 11, 1972. Flocks of ten to twenty migrants are not uncommon. In winter, one or two individuals are seen only occasionally and usually with a small flock of Green-wings.

CINNAMON TEAL. *Anas cyanoptera*

Rare in summer, common in migration, and uncommon in winter. Except for a few summer sightings of lone males at San Vicente on June 9, 1932, at Glenn Springs on June 21, 1928 (Van Tyne and Sutton), and at Rio Grande Village on June 18, 1967 (Wauer), records range from August 19 to May 28. In fall, it is most common along the river from mid-September to early October, and stragglers may be expected to October 19. A high of ninety-one birds was counted in four flocks at Rio Grande Village on October 8, 1970 (Wauer). It is rare during November and December but becomes a regular visitor along the river during January, February, and the first half of March. Spring migrants pass through the area in numbers from March 18 through mid-April, and a few individuals can usually be found in mixed flocks of Green-wings and Blue-wings until mid-May.

AMERICAN WIDGEON. *Mareca americana*

Fairly common migrant and uncommon winter visitor. There also is an August 12, 1967, sighting of a lone female at Rio Grande Village (Wauer). Fall migrants do not reach the Big Bend area until October 18, and a few individuals can sometimes be found along the river and at adjacent ponds throughout the rest of the fall and winter. Spring migrants are most numerous from mid-March to May 16, and there is one late sighting on May 28, 1968.

SHOVELER. *Spatula clypeata*

Common migrant in spring and less numerous in fall. The earliest spring migrant was recorded at Rio Grande Village on February 27, 1971 (Wauer), but the Shoveler is most

numerous from early March through early May; stragglers
and small flocks are not uncommon along the river until mid-
June. A high count of thirty-three birds was recorded at Rio
Grande Village on April 29, 1967 (Wauer). Fall migrants
have been seen as early as September 5 and as late as November 8; there also is a record of a late migrant or winter bird
at Rio Grande Village on December 20, 1969 (Wauer).

WOOD DUCK. *Aix sponsa*

Uncommon fall visitor from October 18 to December 22.
Coleman Newman first saw one of these colorful ducks on
Tornillo Creek, November 7, 1965. Since then it has been
seen regularly along the river and on ponds at Rio Grande
Village, and Easterla found two birds there August 18, 1970.
Most sightings are of single or paired birds, but I found two
pairs at Rio Grande Village on November 10, 1967.

REDHEAD. *Aythya americana*

Rare fall migrant. The first park record is a specimen taken
on the river at San Vicente by Porter on November 2, 1957.
I observed lone birds at Rio Grande Village on November 10,
1967, and on November 22, 1969. Espy has recorded it at
water areas in the Davis Mountains, December through May.

RING-NECKED DUCK. *Aythya collaris*

Uncommon migrant and winter visitor. This diving duck
has been recorded on the river and at adjacent ponds from
October 2 through May 1. One or two individuals are most
common, but on December 27, 1967, I found a "raft" of fifty-
two Ring-necks and two Canvasbacks near Rio Grande Village. They remained throughout the day.

CANVASBACK. *Aythya valisineria*

Sporadic winter visitor. This duck prefers large bodies of
water. It was first observed by Lovie Mae Whitaker at Hot
Springs on December 25, 1939. It was not seen within the
Big Bend Park area again until the latter part of December,

1967, when Siglin found one on the river near Castolon on December 21, and two were seen with Ring-necks at Rio Grande Village on December 27.

LESSER SCAUP. *Aythya affinis*

Rare migrant and winter visitor on the river and adjacent ponds. Records range from October 9 to January 12 and from March 17 to May 28. A specimen was collected near Fort Davis on December 22, 1969 (McDermitt).

COMMON GOLDENEYE. *Bucephala clangula*

There is only one record of this duck within the Big Bend Park area. A female was seen by several observers from December 27, 1969, to January 9, 1970. Keith Olsen saw it first on December 27, Olive W. Evans reported it for January 6, and Sharon Wauer and I saw it on December 28 and January 9.

BUFFLEHEAD. *Bucephala albeola*

Uncommon spring migrant from March 1 to May 1, and recorded on three occasions in November and December. Lone birds were seen on the river near Castolon on November 5, 1967, at Rio Grande Village on November 30, 1968, and near Santa Elena Canyon on December 30, 1968 (Wauer). Although Buffleheads usually occur alone or in twos, I found five near Rio Grande Village on March 7, 1968, and again on May 1, 1970. John C. Yrizany observed eight females on the river on April 8, 1964.

RUDDY DUCK. *Oxyura jamaicensis*

Rare migrant. It has been reported only twice in spring: at Rio Grande Village on March 17, 1969 (Rothstein), and again on April 4, 1967 (Wauer). There are four fall records: Porter collected a bird on the river near San Vicente on October 26, 1957, and I found lone birds at Rio Grande Village on October 10, 1970, November 24, 1966, and November 26, 1967.

HOODED MERGANSER. *Lophodytes cucullatus*

There are only two park records of this little merganser. Porter collected one at Rio Grande Village on December 1, 1958, and the Isleibs found one at Hot Springs on February 4, 1956. It is a rare but regular visitor to water areas near Balmorhea in winter.

COMMON MERGANSER. *Mergus merganser*

There are three park sightings of this duck. Dingus reported one on the river near Boquillas during December, 1964; Shier observed one on a pond at Rio Grande Village on March 16, 1969; and I observed one at Rio Grande Village on February 16, 1971. This species and the Red-breasted Merganser (*Mergus serrator*) are winter visitors on Lake Balmorhea.

AMERICAN VULTURES: Family Cathartidae

TURKEY VULTURE. *Cathartes aura*

Abundant summer resident and migrant. There are records of this scavenger in the park for every month except December, but the only January record is of a lone bird seen north of Persimmon Gap on January 28, 1960. Doug Evans recorded it at Panther Junction as early as February 6, 1965. Regular spring arrivals begin to move into the lowlands the last week of February, and Ruth Jessen reported that her earliest sighting in the Chisos Basin was March 2, 1968.

It is most numerous along the river and in the low mountains during summer, but is also present throughout the high parts of the Chisos Mountains. Murl Deusing found one incubating eggs under a small rocky overhang at Grapevine Hills on March 31, 1970, and immature birds have been seen in the Chisos Basin on a number of occasions during July and August.

By late September it becomes rare in the mountains. Only 2 were seen in Boot Canyon on September 28, 1969, and none were found in the Chisos Basin the following day

(Wauer). Wolf observed a flock of 150 birds moving southeast over the Basin at dusk on August 21, 1968. Fifty-two individuals were seen soaring over Casa Grande at dusk on September 12, 1967 (Wauer). I found 85 birds roosting in cottonwoods at Rio Grande Village on September 26, 1969, and 55 there on October 20, 1967; I could not find these birds early the following morning. One or 2 individuals can usually be found along the river during early November, and the latest sighting is of 2 birds at Rio Grande Village on November 11, 1967 (Frances Williams and John Weske).

BLACK VULTURE. *Coragyps atratus*

Uncommon in summer and winter and fairly common in migration. I have never seen it more than one mile from the river. Black Vultures can usually be found soaring over Rio Grande Village and Santa Elena Crossing during mid-day. It can easily be identified in flight by its rapid wingbeats and broad wings showing white patches near the tips, but perched birds may be more difficult. The all black to gray head and gray legs are good characteristics most of the year. These characteristics are less reliable during late summer, however, when Black Vultures may be found perched alongside young Turkey Vultures that have not yet developed red heads.

Black Vultures assumedly nest within the park, although there are no actual records of nests. I did find two copulating birds at Rio Grande Village on April 5, 1967, and a young bird at Santa Elena Canyon on August 10, 1971. Most sightings are of two or three individuals, but I found eight flying upriver near Boquillas on March 17, 1969, and nine along the river near Castolon on September 2, 1968.

HAWKS, EAGLES, and HARRIERS: Family Accipitridae

SWALLOW-TAILED KITE. *Elanoides forficatus*

There is only one sighting of this large, graceful bird for the park area (Wauer, 1970c). On August 5, 1969, I found

it soaring over Rio Grande Village and was able to take
several photographs during its many passes within an ap-
proximate four-mile area along the Rio Grande. Cecil Gar-
rett also saw it during the morning, Siglin saw it at noon,
and Easterla found it still there in late afternoon. It could
not be found there the following morning.

MISSISSIPPI KITE. *Ictinia misisippiensis*

Rare late spring migrant, and some birds linger at suitable
localities to mid-summer (August 4). An immature bird remained at a pond at Rio Grande Village from June 1 through
July 31, 1968; Guy Anderson photographed an immature
bird at Castolon on June 19, 1970; and three immature birds
were seen at Rio Grande Village from May 29 to June 27,
1971. The Rio Grande Village birds spent most of their day-
light hours perched in the foliage of cottonwood trees. They
would dash out after cicadas, catch them, and eat them in
flight and upon returning to a perch. The aerial acrobatics of
these birds were fascinating to watch. Most park sightings
are of one or two birds along the river from May 4 to June
20. Noberto Ortega and I watched one soaring directly over
Alpine on May 14, 1970. Apparently, this species is a regular spring migrant through the Big Bend Country. It nests in
the vicinity of Balmorhea; Harry Ohlendorf and Tony Mulhagen reported two pairs there in 1970 and found adults
feeding young in 1969.

GOSHAWK. *Accipiter gentilis*

There are three records of this large bird hawk for the
park. It was observed on two separate occasions in 1956: on
July 19, one was seen at Boot Springs by someone recorded
only as Keith, and Jack Burgess reported an immature bird
there in "summer 1956." I have seen it on two occasions over
Boot Canyon: on the evening of August 12, 1967, a lone bird
soared north to south over lower Boot Canyon, and on June
19, 1971, Brent and Becky Wauer and I observed an imma-

ture bird soaring over Boot Canyon for several minutes. I saw it again the following day near the South Rim.

SHARP-SHINNED HAWK. *Accipiter striatus*

Rare summer resident in the mountains, but fairly com mon throughout the park area in migration and during winter. It nested near the top of an Arizona Cypress in Boot Canyon during August, 1966, and on a Mexican Pinyon along the north slope of the top of Emory Peak in June, 1969 (Wauer). As a migrant, it has been recorded from late March to early May and September 15 through mid-November; two birds were banded at Panther Junction on October 28, 1967. Most wintertime records are for the lowlands, although this bird can usually be found in the higher canyons as well. On March 31, 1968, I watched one catch and eat a Rufous-sided Towhee at Laguna Meadow.

COOPER'S HAWK. *Accipiter cooperii*

Fairly common migrant and winter visitor. It is most numerous as a spring and fall migrant from mid-March through May 15 and from September 24 to early November. It has not been recorded within the park from May 16 to August 9, but early migrants appear at the same time as the first southbound warblers reach the area. It is rare during August and most of September but becomes regular toward the end of September. In winter, one or two birds can usually be found almost anywhere in a given day.

RED-TAILED HAWK. *Buteo jamaicensis*

Uncommon summer resident and common migrant and winter resident. Breeding birds are permanent residents throughout most of their range. This is the "Fuertes' Red-tailed Hawk," a very light-colored race, that originally was described in 1935 (Sutton and Van Tyne, 1935) and breeds only in Texas from Brewster County east to Corpus Christi and south through Coahuila and Chihuahua, Mexico. In Big Bend Park, a nest containing one youngster was found near the top of an Arizona Cypress in lower Boot Canyon on May 25, 1967 (Wauer), and the Deusings located a nest on a high cliff at Grapevine Hills, March 27, 1970.

There is no noticeable increase of birds from the north until early November when darker, northern Red-tails reach the area and mingle with resident birds. Many of the visitors remain throughout the winter. Northbound birds begin to pass through the Big Bend by mid-March; this movement of northern individuals continues until early May.

RED-SHOULDERED HAWK. *Buteo lineatus*

There are only two records of this large hawk. I observed lone birds near Santa Elena Canyon on April 2, 1967, and over Tornillo Flat on April 7, 1967.

BROAD-WINGED HAWK. *Buteo platypterus*

Uncommon migrant in spring and rare in fall. It has been reported only since 1966. I have recorded it regularly from March 27 to June 4 in spring. There are four fall sightings: one on August 19, five (two juvenals and three adults) on September 21, one on October 5, 1969, all at Rio Grande Village, and one near Laguna Meadow on September 4, 1966. In spite of the fact that this species migrates in huge flocks in the East, most of the Big Bend sightings are of lone birds.

SWAINSON'S HAWK. *Buteo swainsoni*

Uncommon summer visitor and fairly common migrant from March 8 through December 12. So far as I can find, this species does not nest within the park. It does nest on mesquites and yuccas north of the park and in northern Coahuila and Chihuahua, Mexico, where it is the common breeding Buteo of the mesquite-yucca flatlands. Post-nesting birds visit the park during June and July and are most common along the river, near Persimmon Gap, and near the South Rim. Migrants can be found in flocks of five to ten or more birds and are most numerous from April 8 to 18 in spring. Fall migrants move through the area singly or in pairs and are never as numerous as spring migrants.

ZONE-TAILED HAWK. *Buteo albonotatus*

Uncommon summer resident within the Chisos Mountains and along the Rio Grande canyons. It arrives as early as March 13 and may remain until October 2. Five individuals were detected between Rio Grande Village and Stillwell Crossing during a two-day float trip through Boquillas Canyon on March 22 and 23, 1969 (Wauer). A pair frequents the Rio Grande Village area and often can be found soaring along the limestone ridge just west of the open flats. It nests along the canyon below Hot Springs. Several members of the Texas Ornithological Society observed nest-building on a cliff on the United States side, April 29, 1972. Juvenals can often be seen at Rio Grande Village during July and August. One individual stayed near the large pond behind the store from July 26 to August 22, 1970.

During the summers of 1968, 1969, and 1970, a pair nested in an Emory Oak near Pinnacle Pass east of the Emory Peak Trail; the nest contained two young on June 10, 1969. Another nest, discovered on Crown Mountain by Don Davis on May 7, 1969, contained one egg. The area above Boulder Meadow and along the Boot Canyon Trail below the Emory Peak Trail is the best place to see this bird during summer. It is sometimes found along the base of Campground Canyon in summer as well. Zone-tails often soar along the ridges with Turkey Vultures and may be somewhat confusing because of their very similar appearance. From April to early July, it usually can be located by its high-pitched scream. The banded tail and feathered head easily separate it from the equally dark and bicolor-winged Turkey Vultures.

WHITE-TAILED HAWK. *Buteo albicaudatus*

There are only two records of this southern hawk within the Big Bend area. Adele Harding first saw it over Green Gulch on June 4, 1956, and Jim Court and I watched one as it flew over the Rio Grande from Santa Elena, Chihuahua, to Cottonwood Campground and upriver toward Santa Elena Canyon, April 15, 1967.

ROUGH-LEGGED HAWK. *Buteo lagopus*

There is a single sighting of this northern hawk within the park. I found a lone bird perched on a utility pole near Maverick on December 29, 1967. Although it is rare in the lower part of Brewster County, I have seen it on several occasions in winter along the highway between Marathon and Alpine.

FERRUGINOUS HAWK. *Buteo regalis*

Uncommon migrant and winter visitor as early as October 27 and as late as May 18. It appears that this large hawk is somewhat sporadic in occurrence; it is fairly common some winters and rare others. I found it on a number of occasions during the 1967–68 winter, including eight individuals perched on utility poles along the highway between Marathon and Alpine on November 15. The majority of the park sightings are from the flats between Tornillo Flat and Maverick.

GRAY HAWK. *Buteo nitidus*

There are only two sightings within the park; one bird was seen soaring low over the Rio Grande at Boquillas Crossing, April 14, 1967, and one was found circling Rio Grande Village, April 3, 1970 (Wauer). Nonetheless, it may be a regular spring visitor to the Big Bend Country; for example, one was reported west of Lajitas during the last week of March, 1970, and a dead bird was found in Limpia Canyon in the Davis Mountains by Tony Mulhagen on August 27, 1969.

HARRIS' HAWK. *Parabuteo unicinctus*

Rare summer and winter visitor and migrant. It has been recorded along the Rio Grande near Boquillas and Castolon throughout the year. A nest containing two eggs was found in a mesquite near Nine Point Draw (ten miles south of Persimmon Gap) on August 10, 1964 (Allen and Bruce O'Brian), and I observed a copulating pair of birds south of Marathon on August 20, 1966. It may be a late-nesting bird during some years. Dixon and Wallmo (1956) found it along Highway 385 south of Marathon in 1953, and I have seen it there on a number of occasions. During winters that it resides in the park, it is most likely to be found near Dugout Wells or along the river below Santa Elena Canyon.

BLACK HAWK. *Buteogallus athracinus*

There are but four park records of this hawk, all prior to 1962; I have not seen it in the park. Sutton obtained a specithree occasions—at Rio Grande Village on April 12, 1957, June 26, 1960, and September 27, 1961. The bird probably men at Castolon on May 9, 1935, and Brodrick recorded it on does pass through the Big Bend area in migration because it has nested in Limpia Canyon in the Davis Mountains for several years (Espy).

GOLDEN EAGLE. *Aquila chrysaetos*

Uncommon summer resident and fairly common migrant and winter visitor. At least three pairs of these magnificent birds appear to summer within the park. Pete Koch reported a nest high on Pulliam Ridge's north face that was "used by Golden Eagles for many years." During February and March, 1967, I found a pair in this area on a number of occasions, and a bird of the year was seen nearby on August 24, 1970 (Wauer and Guy Anderson). I believe that a pair also nested near the East Rim in 1968; I observed one bird of the year nearby on June 8. Another pair of Golden Eagles has been seen on a number of occasions near Santa Elena Canyon, and I suspect that they nest somewhere along this long, dissected canyon. Golden Eagles are most commonly seen in migration during February and March and in August and early September.

These large predators hunt their food on the open desert flats; Burro Mesa and the flats to the west and north are excellent localities to find migrant and wintering birds. Their preferred food is rabbit, although they will feed upon anything from road-killed deer to insects. On November 6, 1961, Whitt saw a Golden Eagle with what appeared to be a cottontail in its beak. As the bird circled to gain altitude, a Red-tail overtook it and harassed it in mid-air until the eagle dropped its prey. The Red-tail caught the falling rabbit in mid-air and glided to earth with it. The eagle flew off to find dinner elsewhere.

Van Tyne and Sutton (1937) reported that "local ranchers kill these splendid birds at every opportunity and hang the carcasses from the roadside fences as 'scarecrows' or as evidence of their own prowess." The only change in thirty-four years is that the birds now are seldom displayed along the main roadways. In spite of continued killing, the eagle population apparently has not been appreciably reduced within the park.

BALD EAGLE. *Haliaeetus leucocephalus*

The status of this bird is questionable, but it probably is a rare winter visitor to the Big Bend area. There are only two park sightings: Jim Court saw one flying along the Rio Grande at the Johnson Ranch, November 5, 1967, and Nathan Wallace observed a "mature bird" perched on a snag just south of the upper Tornillo Creek bridge on December 30, 1969. Other Big Bend records include one at the McIvor Upper Ranch in the Davis Mountains by Pansy Espy, Jean McIvor, and Lou C. Evans in spring, 1966, and one on Pine Peak in mid-February, 1970, by Evans; the Millers reported that a specimen was taken on their ranch by biologists from Texas Tech in 1961.

MARSH HAWK. *Circus cyaneus*

Fairly common migrant and uncommon winter visitor. There are two summertime sightings as well, one on Burro

Mesa on June 7, 1955, and one at the South Rim on July 6, 1963 (Brodrick). Summer sightings are probably of non-breeding birds. Fall migrants have been recorded along the river floodplain as early as August 16 but are more numerous from mid-September through October. Spring migrants are fairly common from mid-March through April 14, and stragglers can be found to mid-May. In winter, it is most common along the river, but sightings within the Chisos foothills can be expected.

OSPREYS: Family Pandionidae

OSPREY. *Pandion haliaetus*

Uncommon spring migrant from March 31 through May 16, and rare in fall. Espy found one in the Davis Mountains on September 28, 1968, I observed one at Rio Grande Village the day after a severe rainstorm, September 29, 1970, and another one there on October 3, 1968; Mrs. Cleve Bachman reported a very late bird near Maverick on December 29, 1970. All sightings are of lone individuals along the river or in the desert lowlands, except for one found flying north over Boot Canyon at dusk on March 31, 1967 (Wauer).

CARACARAS and FALCONS: Family Falconidae

CARACARA. *Caracara cheriway*

Rare visitor to the Big Bend area. Van Tyne and Sutton reported that Setzer found a broken humerus of this species in a cave on the south peak of Mule Ears Peaks. Stan Fulcher told me that he and his brother found a nesting pair of these birds in a cottonwood along Terlingua Creek ten miles north of Terlingua in 1922. Van Tyne and Sutton reported that it was "infrequently seen along the Rio Grande in the vicinity of the mouth of Tornillo Creek" prior to 1937. Recent sightings are few and far between; one was seen by the Blocks near Terlingua in June, 1968, and I found one soaring with several Turkey Vultures along the cliffs in Boquillas Canyon on March 22, 1969.

PRAIRIE FALCON. *Falco mexicanus*

Rare summer and winter resident and uncommon migrant. Although I have not found a nest, I watched a pair courting over Mouse Canyon, near Panther Junction, on March 4, 1967, and another courting pair within Mariscal Canyon on April 26, 1969. This bird is most numerous as a spring migrant from early March through May 11. It is rare in fall, but it does winter within the park. I have found it more frequently in the open valleys of the Davis Mountains, where Dave Galland (personal communications) reported "several nesting pairs."

PEREGRINE FALCON. *Falco peregrinus*

Uncommon summer resident and migrant. A pair of these "Duck Hawks" have nested on the high cliffs of the United States side of Boquillas Canyon for several years, although I have not seen fledged birds there. Another pair frequents the western entrance to Mariscal Canyon; I have seen one there on several occasions, and Dick Galland observed a pair on May 13, 1971. Easterla saw a pair at Santa Elena Canyon in early July, 1970, and Brent Wauer and I found a pair and their nest high on the cliff on the Mexican side of Santa Elena Canyon on July 8, 1971; two days later I watched one soaring along the edge of the clifftop, harassing Turkey Vultures perched there. There also have been sightings of paired birds within the Chisos Mountains. Sutton saw what he thought was a mated pair along the west face of Casa Grande on April 27, 1935; more recently, on April 21, 1962, Hardy observed a pair of birds between Toll Mountain and Emory Peak. I found a pair of Peregrines in this same area on May 3, 1967, and saw two young and an adult over Emory Peak on July 21. Pansy Espy and Jody Miller observed a pair feeding young at a nest on a cliff along Limpia Canyon in the Davis Mountains, June 24, 1969.

It appears that the Big Bend Country is one of the last strongholds of this predator that is so high on the food chain. I believe that the isolated mountains and canyons of West Texas may harbor as many as fifteen to twenty-five nesting pairs of these birds.

Peregrines are most often seen during the spring migration from early March to May 8, when they can be expected anywhere within the park, although most sightings are from along the Rio Grande. There is no noticeable fall movement, but park records range from February 25 through November 5; there are no December and January sightings of this bird.

APLOMADO FALCON. *Falco femoralis*

I have searched for this medium-sized falcon ever since I first arrived in the Big Bend. In spite of the fact that a few people have reported seeing it along the River Road and from the South Rim (all these sightings are questionable), I have not been fortunate enough to find it. Apparently, it once did nest within the yucca-grasslands of Big Bend's lowlands. Van Tyne and Sutton reported only one sighting from "along the Rio Grande on the Johnson Ranch," in 1937, and Karl Haller and Pete Koch observed one near Mariscal Mine in February, 1952.

This is a Mexican species that barely reaches the United States in summer. It preys upon insects, lizards, and ground-nesting birds. It is likely that its apparent decline was caused by the destruction and abuse of its preferred habitat during the late 1800's and early 1900's. It is absent or only occasional now throughout its former range in the United States. Although grazing within the park grasslands is officially over, considerable trespass by Mexican stock persists. The chance that the preferred habitat will recover sufficiently for a pair of Aplomado Falcons to find suitable nesting sites within the park area again is doubtful.

PIGEON HAWK. *Falco columbarius*

There are only four park records of this little falcon. Borell

saw one at Laguna Meadow on October 31, 1936; I saw two
at Rio Grande Village on October 26, 1966; Jim Court observed one at Castolon on December 7, 1968; and I observed
one near Panther Junction on January 17, 1971.

SPARROW HAWK. *Falco sparverius*

Uncommon in summer, common in winter, and fairly
common in migration. It is surprisingly hard to find in summer because it nests in rather inaccessible locations. It annually nests along the cliffs east of the South Rim; on May 7,
1967, I found a nest on Crown Mountain in upper Pine Canyon, and two young and an adult were seen along the ridge
just west of Rio Grande Village on July 26, 1969.

It becomes easier to find by late July with the dispersal of
young and adults, but there is no evidence of migration until
early September. A peak is reached in late October, and
stragglers can be found through most of November. Wintering birds are most numerous in the lowlands but can usually
be found along the high ridges and cliffs of the Chisos during
mild days; there is some movement into the adjacent lowlands during stormy periods. Northbound migrants begin to
pass through the Big Bend Country as early as mid-March,
and this movement continues until early May. It is not uncommon to find eight to ten birds perched on Ocotillos and
other tall shrubs during migration.

QUAILS, PHEASANTS, and PEACOCKS:
Family Phasianidae

SCALED QUAIL. *Callipepla squamata*

Common resident below 5,000 feet elevation. This is the
only often-seen quail of the Big Bend Country. Coveys of ten
to forty birds can usually be found along all the park's roadways at dawn and dusk from November through March.
They begin to pair in March, and their tiny, precocial young

can be seen as early as late May. A high count of sixteen young were seen at Panther Junction on June 7, 1971; only six of this clutch were seen July 2 (Wauer). During the very wet spring and summer of 1968, I believe that pairs near Panther Junction produced four broods. Small chicks were seen as late as mid-October.

East Texans call this the "Blue Quail," an appropriate name because of its overall blue-gray color. It also is called "Cottontop" because of the white tuft of feathers on its head.

GAMBEL'S QUAIL. *Lophortyx gambelii*

Extremely rare resident of the Big Bend lowlands. In spite of recent (since 1966) sightings at Maverick, the Old Ranch, Dugout Wells, and along the River Road, I have not seen it within the park. This is the common desert quail of the western deserts, but it becomes quite rare in the Big Bend Country, the eastern edge of its range. Miller reports that it is "cyclic" on his ranch in Jeff Davis County. It probably was never common within the park, and it likely is on the decrease in this area.

HARLEQUIN QUAIL. *Cyrtonyx montezumae*

The status of this species is questionable; it has not been seen within the park for many years. Even as early as 1933, Van Tyne and Sutton considered it to be on the decrease. They wrote (1937) that "local hunters and ranchers testified unanimously to the great decrease in the numbers of this quail in recent years in even remote areas. No adequate explanation of this decrease was offered but surely overgrazing, which now prevails in nearly every part of the country, must be an important contributing factor." The overgrazing in the 1930's and early 1940's, plus the severe drought that hit the Big Bend area during the 1940's and 1950's, probably resulted in the extirpation of this species. Except for a single sighting of a pair of these birds in the Chisos Basin by Adele

Harding, May 19, 1962, there are no records of this bird since the early 1940's.

It does occur in the Del Norte, Glass, and Davis mountains to the north of the park, and in Mexico's southern del Carmens. It can best be found along the roadway in Limpia Canyon in the Davis Mountains. A drive up Limpia Canyon to McDonald Observatory at dusk or dawn often produces a few of these little "fool" or "Mearn's Quail." I have also found it along the entrance road in Davis Mountain State Park.

CHUKAR. *Alectoris graeca*

There are no sightings of this exotic partridge within the park, but a total of 943 birds have been released along the eastern slope of the Dead Horse Mountains not far from the park boundary. The Texas Parks and Wildlife Department released 750 Chukars on the Black Gap Wildlife Management Area in 1958, and 193 birds in 1969 (Tommy L. Hailey). According to an article in the *Alpine Avalanche*, August 28, 1969, the "basic purpose of the stocking is to fill a void in areas where marginal or no native game birds exist." If there are no game birds on a naturally regulated area like the Dead Horse Mountains, it is because none will survive there. I certainly hope that this large, gregarious, and dominant species does not spread to localities within the park where it can eliminate native quail, as it has done within sections of the Panamint Mountains of eastern California.

CRANES: Family Gruidae

SANDHILL CRANE. *Grus canadensis*

Uncommon fall migrant and rare winter visitor. Records of this long-necked bird exist from October 7 through January 24. Except for three birds I found on a sandbar on the river at Rio Grande Village on October 19, 1969, all sightings have been of birds flying overhead. The largest flocks seen were thirteen birds flying south from Croton Peak along the west side of the Chisos Mountains toward Blue Creek, October 15, 1966; twenty-five flying north near Persimmon Gap on February 6, 1971; and thirty-six individuals flying over the river near Boquillas, January 24, 1967 (Sharon Wauer).

RAILS, GALLINULES, and COOTS: Family Rallidae

KING RAIL. *Rallus elegans*

There are two records of this large rail for the park. One of three birds seen at the Rio Grande Village silt pond was collected on August 24, 1969 (Wauer), and Bert Schaughency photographed a lone bird there on April 22, 1970. This is a bird of the fresh-water marshes of the eastern part of the state, and these records suggest that it is a rare migrant along the Rio Grande.

VIRGINIA RAIL. *Rallus limicola*

Rare migrant along the Rio Grande. This bird has been reported for Big Bend Park only in recent years from March 21 through May 11 in spring, and there is one fall sighting; Easterla and Tucker saw one at Rio Grande Village on August 30, 1970. In addition, the Millers recorded it at their ranch on November 14, 1963, and August 30, 1967. As is true for all rails, they are seldom seen, because of their shyness and habitat preference, and this species may be more common than sightings seem to indicate.

SORA. *Porzana carolina*

Rare in summer, fairly common migrant, and uncommon in winter at localized areas adjacent to the Rio Grande. At least one pair was seen or heard calling at the Rio Grande Village silt pond throughout June and July, 1967; I believe that they nested, but I did not see young birds. I could not find Soras at this pond or elsewhere during the summers of

1968, 1969, and 1970. It is most numerous as a migrant from mid-March through May 20, and August 24 through October, when it is easily seen at ponds and at weedy patches along the river. On May 1, 1969, I found six individuals feeding along the runways at the beaver pond off the Rio Grande Village Nature Trail; on September 13, 1967, I watched seven Soras "grazing" along the bank of the silt pond; and eight individuals were seen at Rio Grande Village on September 19, 1969. A few remain throughout the winter and can usually be detected at the silt pond or beaver pond with a little squeaking and loud handclaps.

PURPLE GALLINULE. *Porphyrula martinica*

There are only two records of this colorful rail for the park. I first found one foraging along the runways at the Rio Grande Village beaver pond on April 20, 1967, and called it to the attention of Hanlon, McCarroll, Meyer, Kuehn, and Rowe, who were birding in the area. I found what I assumed to be the same bird on April 25 and May 1 at the same location. A second record is one seen at the Rio Grande Village Campground pond on June 30, 1970. It was seen first by Lauri Miller and Bill Jensen and later the same morning by Easterla and the Hotchkisses, who photographed the bird. It remained at this pond until July 3. This late record is especially interesting because on June 29 more than two inches of rain fell at Rio Grande Village from a storm that had come from the north. I cannot help but wonder what this southern bird was doing at this location.

COMMON GALLINULE. *Gallinule chloropus*

Rare migrant along the river. It first was reported for the park by David and Roy Brown, who observed two birds at Rio Grande Village on April 27, 1966. It has since been found on a few occasions from April 20 to May 29 in spring, and from September 30 to October 15 in fall. Only once have I found more than a lone individual—two at Rio Grande Village on May 3, 1970.

AMERICAN COOT. *Fulica americana*

Rare in summer, fairly common in migration, and uncommon in winter along the river and at adjacent ponds. It nested at the Rio Grande Village silt pond during the summers of 1967, 1970, and 1971, but I did not find it in the summers of 1968 and 1969. The pond was dredged to deepen the channel in 1967 and 1970, but not in the intervening years, which suggests that the ecological requirements for the Coot, as well as for the Sora and Pied-billed Grebe, include an open pond with nearby concealment. In migration it occurs singly or in small flocks; the largest number of birds recorded was fourteen at Rio Grande Village on October 27, 1966. Spring migrants pass through the area from mid-March through May; I have detected peaks in movements in late March and early May. Fall migrants are more regular and appear from early October through mid-November. Wintering birds can usually be found at ponds, but they are rare in the riverway itself.

PLOVERS: Family Charadriidae

SEMIPALMATED PLOVER. *Charadrius semipalmatus*

There is but one park record of this species. Two birds were found on a small mud bank of the Rio Grande just upriver from the Boquillas Crossing on April 26, 1970 (Wauer). Plovers are rare within the lower part of the Big Bend, but this species, Snowy Plover (*Charadrius alexandrinus*), and Mountain Plover (*Eupoda montana*) are seen regularly in migration in the vicinity of Balmorhea.

KILLDEER. *Charadrius vociferus*

Uncommon in summer, and fairly common in migration and during the winter at appropriate localities below 5,000 feet elevation. Most sightings are along the river and at Rio Grande Village and Castolon. Three fledged young were seen at the Rio Grande Village sewage lagoon on May 24, 1969

(Wauer). In migration it can be expected anywhere, including the open desert. Spring migrants are most numerous from mid-March through May 24, and fall migrants pass through the area between August 12 and early October.

WOODCOCKS, SNIPES, and SANDPIPERS:
Family Scolopacidae

AMERICAN WOODCOCK. *Philohela minor*

There is only one record of this bird for the park. Coleman Newman and Dan Beard found two individuals along an irrigation ditch at Rio Grande Village on November 2, 1965.

COMMON SNIPE. *Capella gallinago*

Uncommon migrant and winter visitor. Records of this snipe range from August 31 through May 11, but it is most numerous as a fall migrant from October 15 to November 5. A few can usually be found at pond edges and irrigation ditches at Rio Grande Village and Cottonwood Campground all winter. There is a slight increase in numbers toward the end of March as spring migrants pass through the area. This northbound movement, which is not as great as that in the fall, subsides by mid-April, but stragglers continue to be seen until May 11. Most records are of lone birds, but I found twelve together at Rio Grande Village on September 29, 1970.

LONG-BILLED CURLEW. *Numenius americanus*

Uncommon migrant. It first was observed by Lovie Mae Whitaker at Hot Springs in September, 1935. Doug Evans and Bruce Shaw observed and photographed one on Tornillo Flat on May 27, 1964. It has since been found from March 16 to May 21 in spring, and from August 25 to September 12 in fall. Two or three birds are most usual, but Dick Strange saw a flock of eight at Rio Grande Village on April 14, 1965, and I found seven there on April 11, 1967. This long-legged shorebird prefers open, grassy areas and is seldom seen along the river.

WHIMBREL. *Numenius phaeopus*

There are only two records of this curlew for the Big Bend area. One was reported near Panther Junction on April 27. 1957 (Brodrick), and Robert M. La Val saw one along Tornillo Creek at Hot Springs on April 26, 1969. He reported it to me, and I found it still present there two days later. It was collected and represents the first specimen of this species for West Texas.

UPLAND SANDPIPER. *Bartramia longicauda*

Rare fall migrant, and there is a single spring sighting of a lone bird at Rio Grande Village on May 11, 1970 (Wauer). The first park record was of two birds at Rio Grande Village on August 14, 1968, by John W. Corn. He photographed the birds and sent me the photographs as documentation (Wauer, 1970a). It has since been seen on a number of occasions between August 12 and 30 at Rio Grande Village. On August 28, 1970, Judge Charlie Shannon saw one in the Park Headquarters parking area. He told me about the bird and we soon found it. Judge Shannon said that it once was a fairly common migrant around Marfa, but that he rarely hears them pass overhead now. Two days later, Easterla and Tucker found twelve individuals at an irrigated field at Rio Grande Village. This species is usually called "Upland Plover," but that name is misleading, since it is not a plover.

SPOTTED SANDPIPER. *Actitis macularia*

Common migrant and winter resident along the river and at adjacent ponds. Except for a brief period from June 13 to July 16, it has been found throughout the year. Fall migrants reach a peak from mid-August until the last of September. and northbound birds are most numerous from mid-March through May 21. Migrants occur at stock ponds throughout the desert, and one was seen in the Chisos Basin at the sewage lagoons on September 15, 1968 (Wauer). In winter it can be seen almost anywhere along the river; I found more than thirty birds while rafting through Mariscal Canyon on February 1, 1968.

SOLITARY SANDPIPER. *Tringa solitaria*

Fairly common migrant and somewhat sporadic in occurrence. Spring records range from March 23 to May 10, fall sightings from July 15 to October 12. Migrants are not restricted to the river but can be expected anywhere below 4,000 feet; there are several sightings from Maverick and Panther Junction. Most records are of lone birds, but a flock of seven was seen at Rio Grande Village on August 5, 1969 (Wauer).

WILLET. *Catoptrophorus semipalmatus*

Rare migrant. There are three spring sightings: Alexander Sprunt, Jr., observed one in the Chisos Basin on March 15, 1950; Bob Barbee found three at Rio Grande Village on April 9, 1967; and I found one there on April 11, 1969. There are two fall sightings: I found sixteen birds bathing along the river at Rio Grande Village on August 15, 1969; John Mac-Donald and Tom Myer reported one there on August 19, 1970. This is a common migrant at Lake Balmorhea.

GREATER YELLOWLEGS. *Totanus melanoleucus*

Fairly common migrant along the Rio Grande and adjacent ponds. It has been recorded from March 17 to April 13 in spring, and from July 14 to October 15 in fall. There is a late spring sighting at Rio Grande Village on May 20, 1968 (Wauer).

LESSER YELLOWLEGS. *Totanus flavipes*

Uncommon migrant from April 1 through May 11 in spring and from July 17 to October 26 in fall. Lone birds may be expected at old stock ponds on the desert as well as along the river, and five were seen at a flooded field at Rio Grande

Village on September 16, 1970 (Wauer). There also is one winter sighting; the Isleibs found it at Rio Grande Village from February 3 to 5, 1965.

KNOT. *Calidris canutus*

There is a single record of this bird for the park area. I observed one at a pond at Rio Grande Village on September 3, 1966.

BAIRD'S SANDPIPER. *Erolia bairdii*

Rare migrant and winter visitor. Van Tyne and Sutton first recorded this species in April and May, 1935, and collected a specimen at Lajitas on May 10. I found two along the river at Rio Grande Village on April 15, 1971, and Jim Tucker found two birds at the sewage lagoon in the Chisos Basin on May 10, 1969. Fall records range from July 26 to November 8: Warren Pulich found six individuals at the Green Valley Ranch, north of the park, on July 26, 1961, and I collected a bird at Rio Grande Village on September 2, 1967, and saw lone birds there on September 29, 1970, and November 8, 1969. Two winter sightings include one at Hot Springs in January, 1963 (Woolfenden), and twelve there on January 1, 1965 (Dingus).

LEAST SANDPIPER. *Erolia minutilla*

Fairly common migrant and uncommon winter visitor along the river and at adjacent water areas. This is the most numerous of Big Bend's "peeps." It has been recorded every month but May and June. Spring sightings range from mid-March to April 23; a high count of twelve birds was seen near the Boquillas Crossing on April 5, 1970 (Wauer). Fall migrants reach the Big Bend area as early as July 14, and this bird can be expected at suitable places throughout the fall and winter. I have seen it regularly in winter along lower Tornillo Creek, at Hot Springs, and along Calamity Creek just south of Alpine on Highway 118.

LONG-BILLED DOWITCHER. *Limnodromus scolopaceus*

There are only four sightings of Dowitchers within the park, but only one positive record of a Long-bill. Dave Snyder heard and observed one from only a few yards away at Cottonwood Campground on August 27, 1971. Interestingly enough, two sightings were on the same day of the year; one at Hot Springs on December 30, 1967 (Ribble and Black), and one at Rio Grande Village on December 30, 1969 (Wauer). Mr. and Mrs. O. J. Theobald observed one at Rio Grande Village on April 15, 1971. This species apparently is a common migrant in the vicinity of Lake Balmorhea; Scudday collected four individuals there on April 6, 1967.

WESTERN SANDPIPER. *Ereunetes mauri*

Rare migrant and winter visitor. There is only one spring sighting; Van Tyne and Sutton saw three birds feeding along the river at Lajitas on May 10, 1935. I have found fall migrants at Rio Grande Village on three occasions: two on September 3 and four on September 10, 1966, and two on September 6, 1967. There are but two winter records, at Rio Grande Village on December 8 and 27, 1968 (Wauer).

AVOCETS and STILTS: Family Recurvirostridae

AMERICAN AVOCET. *Recurvirostra americana*

Uncommon spring migrant and rare in fall. Spring sightings range from April 10 through May 29. Although most records are from the vicinity of the river, the Hotchkisses found eight individuals along the roadway near Todd Hill on May 29, 1970. A high count of thirty birds was reported from Rio Grande Village by Roy and David Brown on April 27, 1966. Fall records include fifteen birds seen along the river between Castolon and Santa Elena Canyon on September 24, 1967, and one at Rio Grande Village on October 6, 1970 (Wauer); Easterla saw one south of the park at a pond near Las Norias, Coahuila, Mexico, August 10, 1970.

BLACK-NECKED STILT. *Himantopus mexicanus*

There are only three park records of this long-legged wader. I found lone birds at Rio Grande Village on October 3, 1968, March 23, 1971, and April 22, 1970. The Clay Millers report the bird to be a "regular migrant" on their ranch, and it is fairly common in spring and fall at Lake Balmorhea.

PHALAROPES: Family Phalaropodidae

WILSON'S PHALAROPE. *Steganopus tricolor*

Rare migrant. It appears that this species may have decreased in numbers during recent years. Van Tyne and Sutton recorded it three times during May, 1935, but I have found it only three times in four years: lone birds were seen on ponds at Rio Grande Village on September 20, 1966, and May 1 and 6, 1970. Warren Pulich reported one from Green Valley Ranch, north of the park, on July 28, 1961. There also is a record of the Northern Phalarope (*Lobipes lobatus*) for the Big Bend area. Scudday collected one at Lake Balmorhea on October 21, 1969.

GULLS and TERNS: Family Laridae

RING-BILLED GULL. *Larus delawarensis*

There are but two sightings in the park. Felix Hernandez and I saw four individuals (three adults and one juvenal) resting on a sandbar near Boquillas Crossing on April 26, 1968, and the Blocks found one at Hot Springs on March 9, 1969. Additional sightings include a lone bird ten miles south of Marathon along Highway 385 on October 23, 1969 (Wauer); it has been recorded at Lake Balmorhea regularly in fall, winter, and spring.

LAUGHING GULL. *Larus atricilla*

There is a single record of this gull for the Big Bend; Thompson (1953) found a dead bird at an earthen tank at Black Gap in June, 1951.

FRANKLIN'S GULL. *Larus pipixcan*

There are four records for the Big Bend Park area. Alexander Sprunt, Jr., first saw one at Hot Springs on June 15, 1956. I found lone birds north of Persimmon Gap on two occasions in 1969: near the Leary Ranch on October 23, and two miles north of the park entrance on November 13. On the very windy morning of April 14, 1971, I observed twenty-nine black-and-white gulls flying together up Tornillo Creek, near the lower bridge, at about 7:00 A.M. At 10:30 A.M. the same morning, Dick Brownstein, Ed Seeker, Paul Benham, and Joe Grzybowski found twenty-nine Franklin's Gulls flying north about twenty miles south of Marathon. If both sightings are of the same twenty-nine gulls, they traveled about fifty-five miles in three and one-half hours.

LEAST TERN. *Sterna albifrons*

There is only one record for the park; Maxilla Evans observed a lone bird flying over the Rio Grande at Talley, just west of Mariscal Canyon, on April 4, 1969. It apparently is more common than the lone sighting indicates, however, because Pansy Espy has recorded it in February, June, and September in the Davis Mountains.

PIGEONS and DOVES: Family Columbidae

BAND-TAILED PIGEON. *Columba fasciata*

Fairly common summer resident and sporadic winter resident in the Chisos Mountains. It may first be detected by its owllike *oo-whoo* call, which may be rather ventriloquistic within the narrow canyons. It usually can be found in Boot and Pine canyons throughout the year, but it visits lower canyons during periods of good acorn crops. A high of seventy birds was found in Boot Canyon on August 8, 1969 (Wauer). In July and August of 1969 and 1970 it could be found in numbers in the oak groves along the Window Trail. Walter

Rooney, who lived at Oak Creek (just below the Window) from 1916 to 1923, told Doug Evans (National Park Service files) that "millions of pigeons" came into Oak Creek for a mile "like the wind blowing" when the acorns were on the trees. One pigeon that was killed had twenty-eight acorns in it. Apparently, an occasional bird may move out of the mountains altogether in fall; Charles Bender saw one at Dugout Wells on August 21, 1966. On May 11, 1968, I found five birds feeding among the oaks at 4,800 feet in lower Green Gulch.

In winter it appears to be common at times but very difficult to find at others. On December 23, 1968, Christmas Bird Counters Siglin and Nelson counted fifty-eight individuals in Boot Canyon. I found it common there on January 27 and February 22, 1968, and again on March 9, 1969, but I did not find a single Band-tail there on January 28 and 29, 1967. It is also sporadic in winter in the Davis Mountains, according to Wildlife Conservation Officer Harvey Adams. I have seen it near the roadway in Madera Canyon in November, December, and January.

ROCK DOVE. *Columba livia*

This is the domestic pigeon of American suburbs. It has been recorded within the park only twice, although it is common at towns in northern Brewster County. Cecilia Davis found a lone bird in the patio at Park Headquarters, Panther Junction, June 10, 1970. Lauri Miller attended to its food necessities, and the bird remained for several days. The only other park record was on June 24, 1970; Easterla saw a Peregrine capture one of two Rock Doves over Rio Grande Village.

WHITE-WINGED DOVE. *Zenaida asiatica*

Fairly common permanent resident at mesquite thickets along the river, in adjacent washes, at springs below 5,000 feet elevation, and locally within the lower canyons of the

Chisos Mountains. Lowland birds begin to pair early in February, and the earliest *who-cooks-for-whoo* call was heard on February 14. One nest was found on a branch of an Emory Oak along the Window Trail, May 11, 1968, another was found forty-five feet above the ground on the branch of a huge cottonwood at Boquillas on May 21, 1968, and two juvenals were frightened from a nest in lower Blue Creek Canyon on June 8, 1971 (Wauer). Nesting continues into July; I found a pair building a nest at Rio Grande Village on July 18, 1970. They are most difficult to find during the latter part of the nesting period.

In winter the birds flock at preferred areas, such as Rio Grande Village (I found seventy individuals there on January 22, 1970), Dugout Wells, Panther Junction (I found twenty-two birds there on November 10, 1967), and along the Window Trail. The majority, if not all, of Big Bend Park's White-wings are resident; one banded at Panther Junction on April 23, 1968, was recaptured there on February 3 and June 6, 1969. The park's White-wings are considered to be of the "Mexican Highland" race of central Mexico and the lower Big Bend Country, according to Cottam and Trefethen's (1968) very thorough analysis, *The Life History, Status and Management of the White-winged Dove.*

MOURNING DOVE. *Zenaidura macroura*

Common summer resident and migrant, and fairly common winter resident along the river floodplain, at springs, and in washes and canyons below 5,000 feet elevation. Some birds are permanent residents. For example, birds banded at Panther Junction include one banded on April 6, 1967, and recaptured on April 13 and December 8, 1969, another banded on January 22 and recaptured on May 25, 1968, and January 30, 1969, and one banded on March 26 and recaptured on December 2, 1968.

Nesting occurs from March through June most years, much later during wet years. During the fall of 1966, a nest with one egg was found on a cottonwood at Rio Grande Village as late as September 17 (Wauer). Wintering birds are usually in small flocks of ten to twenty individuals.

GROUND DOVE. *Columbigallina passerina*

Uncommon summer resident and migrant, and sporadic in winter at a few localities. It nests in mesquite thickets along the river and adjacent flats, like those at Rio Grande Village, where it was found nest-building on June 23, 1969, and incubating two eggs on September 7, 1968 (Wauer). It is most common in migration from March 20 through May in spring, and from mid-August through October in fall. Sightings away from the vicinity of the Rio Grande are few; a lone bird was seen at Panther Junction on April 6, 1967, and one was banded there on September 1, 1969. In winter it usually is present in small numbers on open weedy and mesquite flats along the river (I found seven near Castolon on January 25, 1969), but apparently it is sporadic in occurrence. I could not find a single bird during the cool, dry winter of 1969–70.

INCA DOVE. *Scardafella inca*

Rare summer visitor and uncommon migrant. This little dove apparently has decreased in numbers in recent years. Van Tyne and Sutton (1937) found it "almost daily at Castolon . . . inhabiting the mesquite bordering and cultivated fields." It favors areas of human habitation and breeds at Mexican dwellings and villages across the river; Tarleton Smith reported it feeding with chickens at Boquillas during June and July, 1936. I found it breeding within the park only once—a copulating pair at Rio Grande Village on May 7, 1971. Most of the summertime sightings at Castolon and Rio Grande Village probably are visitors from across the river. It is most common in migration from March 27 to May 20 in spring, and from August 6 through early November in fall.

WHITE-FRONTED DOVE. *Leptotila verreauxi*

There are only three park sightings of this southern species. It was first reported from Dugout Wells and the Chisos Basin by Alexander Sprunt, Jr., June 10 and 12, 1956. I found a lone bird at Rio Grande Village on June 30, 1970.

CUCKOOS, ROADRUNNERS, and ANIS:
Family Cuculidae

YELLOW-BILLED CUCKOO. *Coccyzus americanus*

Fairly common summer resident at cottonwood groves along the Rio Grande, such as those at Rio Grande Village and Cottonwood Campground, and less common at riparian areas up to 5,500 feet elevation. On June 30, 1971, I heard one calling in lower Boot Canyon. This is one of the last summer residents to arrive on its breeding grounds. H. T. Hargis recorded it as early as April 27; it may stay as late as September 24 but becomes quite scarce by August 20. Nesting records (all at Rio Grande Village) include two nests found on cottonwoods on June 8, 1969, and one containing one egg on a mesquite on July 23, 1968; an adult was seen feeding a cicada to a nestling on July 31 (Wauer). On September 8, 1969, I observed a Roadrunner with a recently captured young Yellow-billed Cuckoo. This bird is locally called a "rain crow," because it is said that it is noisier just before rain.

ROADRUNNER. *Geococcyx californianus*

Fairly common resident in the lowlands and less so up to 5,500 feet elevation. I know of no better place to find this ground cuckoo than at Rio Grande Village, where it is numerous. Courting begins in February; the first "bark" of the season was heard at Rio Grande Village on February 15, 1968 (Wauer), and nest-building was taking place in mid-March. I found one egg laid in a nest there on March 20. Other nesting records include one nest with three eggs there on March 31, 1970 (Deusing), one with three eggs near the

Chisos Basin sewage lagoon on May 25, 1969, one with three eggs and three young at Rio Grande Village on June 19, 1968, and one with two young ready to leave the nest there on August 5, 1969.

GROOVE-BILLED ANI. *Crotophaga sulcirostris*

This species appears to be increasing in West Texas. Park records range from April 20 through October 9. The first record for the Trans-Pecos was one collected north of the park at Black Gap by W. F. Blair in June, 1951 (Thompson, 1953). Siglin saw one at Rio Grande Village and watched it for several minutes before it flew across the river on August 4, 1967. On May 21, 1968, one of two birds seen at Rio Grande Village was collected, and its status in Texas was discussed by Wauer (1968*b*). Since these first records, it has become a regular summer visitor at Rio Grande Village and the adjacent floodplain, arriving in late June and remaining until early October; two were seen there on October 9, 1971 (Wauer). Although there are no records of a successful nesting, a pair built a nest along the Rio Grande Village Nature Trail on July 26, 1969; they deserted this nest within a few days but constructed two more in a cottonwood at the pond next to the campground, August 5 to 12. These nests were deserted as well. An additional sighting is one at the Clay Miller Ranch by the Millers and Espy on November 10, 1969.

BARN OWLS: Family Tytonidae

BARN OWL. *Tyto alba*

The status of this species is questionable. It has been recorded only a few times from March 1 to May 24, and Allen found one at Devil's Den on September 9, 1963. Although the Barn Owl usually is considered to be resident, it apparently is a rare migrant through the park. Recent sightings include lone birds at Rio Grande Village on March 1, 1963 (the Bedells), March 20, 1969 (Baille and Sparrow), and

May 24, 1968 (Wauer). I found another lone bird at Cotton-wood Campground on March 24, 1969.

TYPICAL OWLS: Family Strigidae

SCREECH OWL. *Otus asio*

Fairly common permanent resident. Although it is seldom seen, it can be heard calling from thickets of mesquite and willows along the river and from pinyon-juniper-oak woodlands in the mountains almost any night from late fall through early spring. Both the "bouncing-ball" call of the typical western Screech Owl and the long, quavering whistle of the eastern Screech Owl can be heard. Joe Marshall (1967) found that the Big Bend area represents the only North American area of overlap of the two birds. Subspecies *suttoni* and *mccalli* hybridize there. Marshall found a mixed pair with grown young at Boquillas in July, 1962. In 1967, I found an adult carrying food to a hole in a large willow tree at Boquillas on June 8; Brodrick found a pair with three youngsters at the K-Bar Ranch on June 29, 1960; and Easterla observed two adults feeding young at Boot Springs on July 9, 1968.

FLAMMULATED OWL. *Otus flammeolus*

Fairly common summer resident at localized highland areas. Park records range from March 30 to September 24. It has been found most often in Boot Canyon, where a juvenal was seen with a captured monarch butterfly on June 8, 1968 (Wauer). During April and May it usually can be called up right after dark with a few hoots that need sound only partially like the deep *boot* call of this bird. One must stay overnight at Boot Springs, however, to be assured of seeing the Flammulated Owl. It begins its nightly activities about one hour after sunset—at approximately 9:00 to 9:15 P.M. in May and June—and usually can be found in the main canyon just beyond the cabin. It also has been seen on the north slope of Casa Grande on two occasions; N. C. Hazard photographed one there on April 19, 1965, and Dave and Ginger Harwood saw two birds there on April 20, 1970.

GREAT HORNED OWL. *Bubo virginianus*

Fairly common summer and winter resident and migrant below 5,500 feet elevation. This is the regularly seen large owl of the river canyons, floodplain, and desert springs. It is likely that most of the park's birds are permanent residents, but there is a distinct increase in sightings from March 22 to May 26 and from early September through November 23.

PYGMY OWL. *Glaucidium gnoma*

There are only two records of this tiny owl. I heard lone birds call at Boot Springs at dawn on August 10 and September 28, 1969. These records constitute the second and third records for Texas, but additional birds should be expected for the Chisos Mountains. Miller (1955) found the Pygmy Owl to be present in pine-oak habitats at 7,000 feet elevation in the Sierra del Carmens of Mexico. Since this area is less than fifty miles from the Chisos Mountains, Big Bend's Pygmy Owls may be post-nesting visitors from that area.

ELF OWL. *Micrathene whitneyi*

Fairly common summer resident and migrant below 5,600 feet elevation. Park records range from March 16 through September 12. It apparently migrates along the river, because it is common there first, arriving at Panther Junction in another five to eight days; the earliest Chisos Basin record is April 17. Early birds are very vociferous and call from "posts" along the edges of their territories. By mid- or late April, however, when their territories have been defined and nesting has begun, they become quieter and are more difficult to find.

Quillin (1935) found the Elf Owl nesting in Juniper Canyon on May 21, 1934. Two or three pairs utilize the Rio

Grande Village area; it usually can be found at Dugout Wells; at least three pairs nest at Panther Junction (a pair has nested in a telephone pole behind Park Headquarters annually from 1967 through 1972); and several pairs nest along the Window Trail and near the Basin Amphitheatre. By late June the birds become very quiet but can often be found at night hunting moths around lights at Park Headquarters and in the Chisos Basin. They also are sometimes seen along the park roads, where they suddenly fly up alongside a passing automobile. I have found family groups in mesquite thickets after nesting as well: three individuals at Dugout Wells on July 4, 1968, and three there on August 17, 1968. The status of this little owl within the southwestern United States was recently summarized by Barlow and Johnson (1967).

BURROWING OWL. *Speotyto cunicularia*

Rare summer resident and migrant. There are only a few sightings of this diurnal owl for the park, but it is more common in open fields from Fort Davis to Balmorhea and east to Sanderson. Van Tyne and Sutton first reported it from Glenn Springs on June 27, 1928, and from Castolon on May 9, 1935. More recently, a pair was seen at a burrow near the Loop Camp turnoff on the River Road, April 17, 1969; an apparent migrant was found at Rio Grande Village on November 2, 1969 (Wauer); and Steve Williams saw one near the Fossil Bone Display on April 9, 1971.

LONG-EARED OWL. *Asio otus*

Rare summer resident in the mountains and rare migrant and winter visitor. It probably nests at Boot Springs, where I heard it calling on June 11, 1967, and June 7, 1970. Additional records include a specimen taken by Borell at Neville Spring on November 29, 1936, and a lone bird seen near San Vicente on May 10, 1933 (Van Tyne and Sutton). Espy recorded it in the Davis Mountains only during December, and Jody Miller found a dead bird at the Miller Ranch on April 22, 1961.

SHORT-EARED OWL. *Asio flammeus*

There are only two records of this owl for the park; I found a lone bird at Dugout Wells on April 27, 1968, and Charles Crabtree observed five or six individuals at Rice Tank on January 4, 1971. Scudday collected one eleven miles east of Lake Balmorhea on January 29, 1969, and the Clay Millers recorded it at their ranch in December, 1955, and on November 1 and 16, 1959. It may be more common within the northern portion of the Big Bend Country than these few records indicate.

SAW-WHET OWL. *Aegolius acadicus*

There are but two park records of this bird. I first heard one calling near Boot Springs after dark on November 3, 1967, but I could not call it close enough for a good look Then, on February 23, 1968, one was taken from a mist net at Boot Springs (Wauer, 1969*b*). It may be a winter visitor from the Sierra del Carmens of Coahuila, Mexico, where Easterla found it to be breeding in July, 1970.

GOATSUCKERS: Family Caprimulgidae

WHIP-POOR-WILL. *Caprimulgus vociferus*

Fairly common summer resident in high mountain canyons and along north slopes above 5,700 feet elevation, and rare to 5,300 feet. Park records range from April 2 to September 23. Most sightings are from Boot and Pine canyons, but birds often can be heard along the Lost Mine Trail and near Juniper Flat. Two juvenals and an adult were found in lower Boot Canyon on June 17, 1971 (Wauer), and Steve Van Pelt found a nest, with one spotted youngster, on a steep oak-covered slope at 5,300 feet on the east side of Ward Mountain, July 19, 1970. Although these birds are very vociferous before the breeding period, they are quiet during nestings and may be almost entirely silent, except for dusk and dawn songs, by late July.

POOR-WILL. *Phalaenoptilus nuttallii*

Fairly common summer resident, common migrant, and rare in winter. There are records of this small goatsucker every month, but only one each for December, January, and February. By the middle of March it can be found along all the park roads below 4,500 feet elevation. Migrants pass through the area from April 25 through May in spring, and from early September through October 26 in fall. Seven individuals were counted on the road between Panther Junction and Dugout Wells on October 10, 1970 (Wauer). In summer it is most common on open desert flats and below the pinyon-juniper-oak woodlands, but a few utilize higher slopes and ridges; Poor-wills were heard calling from the open, southern side of the Emory Peak ridge at 7,000 feet on June 8 and 11, 1968 (Wauer).

COMMON NIGHTHAWK. *Chordeiles minor*

Uncommon spring migrant and rare in fall. There is no indication that this bird nests within the park, but it is resident in summer north of the park in the Del Norte, Davis, and Glass mountains. Spring migrants pass through the area from April 22 to May 26, after which there are no sightings until July 4, when post-nesting birds may be occasional visitors along the river. The fall migration is sparse and lasts from late July to September 24.

LESSER NIGHTHAWK. *Chordeiles acutipennis*

Common summer resident and migrant. It occurs almost everywhere below 4,000 feet elevation in summer, but is most numerous along the floodplain and in adjacent washes, where its hoarse *purring* can be heard as a low roar at dawn. It does not reach the Big Bend area until April 4 and becomes abundant from mid-April to May 27. On May 25, 1971, I found two eggs beneath a small Creosotebush near San Vicente. Summering birds depart by late August, but southbound birds can usually be found along the river until October 18. Migrants have been recorded at Boot Springs and the

South Rim, and Allen observed a flock of fifty-one individuals north of Persimmon Gap on August 17, 1963.

SWIFTS: Family Apodidae

CHIMNEY SWIFT. *Chaetura pelagica*

There are two records of this bird for the park. I observed and heard two individuals calling to one another over Hot Springs on April 27, 1968, and found a lone bird over Rio Grande Village on April 28, 1969. Apparently, this species is increasing its range, as I have seen it a number of times in summer in Odessa, Texas. In 1956, Wolfe regarded it as a summer resident of Texas only west to Travis and Bexar counties.

WHITE-THROATED SWIFT. *Aeronautes saxatalis*

Common summer resident and migrant and uncommon in winter. In summer, it can be found almost anywhere high cliffs exist, from the river canyons to the top of Emory Peak in the Chisos Mountains. It also spends considerable time foraging over the open desert flats. Spring migrants move through the area from late March through May, but fall migrants are less conspicuous, although a flock of sixty to seventy-five birds was seen over Panther Junction on July 27, 1968 (Wauer). Wintering birds can often be found at the river canyons on mild days. Seventy-five birds were counted at Santa Elena Canyon on December 22, 1967, and forty-five were seen near Boquillas Canyon on December 30, 1969 (Wauer). This species also has a wintertime roost in a cave under the South Rim.

HUMMINGBIRDS: Family Trochilidae

LUCIFER HUMMINGBIRD. *Calothorax lucifer*

Fairly common spring, summer, and fall resident. It arrives as early as March 8 and has been recorded as late as November 10. This species previously has been considered to be quite rare within the Big Bend, the only place within the United States where it has been recorded regularly. It can be quite numerous, however. In May, except for the Black-chinned Hummer on the floodplain, it may be the humming-bird most commonly seen from the Rio Grande to the highest slopes of the Chisos Mountains. And when Century Plants are in bloom, usually from May through September, Luci-fers can be found at almost any plant.

It apparently nests in a wide range of habitats. Warren and Bobby Pulich (1963) found it nesting on a Lechuguilla stalk on the open desert near Terlingua, July 13, 1962, a record that was the first for the United States. Dick Nelson (1970) reported a nest found on May 18, 1968, at 5,000 feet elevation near the Basin Campground. I found an immature bird, barely able to fly, in lower Blue Creek Canyon on June 8, 1971, and very young birds were observed at a feeder at my home at Panther Junction the first week of August, 1969. An adult female had been using the feeder since late May. Hummingbird feeders at Panther Junction are the fastest and easiest places in the park to find this Mexican species from early April to mid-September.

Post-nesting birds frequent the mountain canyons; eight males and seven females were counted in Boot Canyon on August 9, 1969 (Wauer). By late August highland birds be-gin to move into the lowlands and can usually be found in the lower canyons until the second week of September, when there is a noticeable decrease in sightings. From early Octo-ber to November they are most often seen in the lower parts of the desert and along the floodplain, where they frequent areas with flowering Tree Tobacco plants.

RUBY-THROATED HUMMINGBIRD. *Archilochus colubris*

Rare migrant and post-nesting visitor. There are two spring sightings only, both at Rio Grande Village; adult males were seen on May 6, 1970 (Wauer), and on May 11, 1969 (Jim Cameron). Fall records include a lone male that appeared at my feeder at Panther Junction on August 23, 1969, and remained until September 1. Another male was seen at Rio Grande Village on September 1, 1969; Pete Sanchez and I saw one at 6,300 feet elevation near the Emory Peak Trail junction, October 5, 1968; and I found another male near Castolon on October 19. This species may be more common than the few records indicate; it is next to impossible to identify females in the field, and males are easily overlooked.

BLACK-CHINNED HUMMINGBIRD. *Archilochus alexandri*

Common summer resident and migrant. It has been recorded every month but January and February. Black-chins arrive the second week of March and immediately begin to nest on cottonwoods and mesquites along the river. Two eggs had already hatched in a nest located at the Boquillas Crossing, April 18, 1970; two young were ready to leave the nest on May 4 and were gone May 6 (Wauer). It apparently nests throughout the summer; I found a nest with two eggs at Rio Grande Village on June 12, 1970, and a young bird still in the nest in Panther Canyon (4,200 feet elevation) on August 12, 1967.

Males begin to move into the Chisos foothills by late March, and by early June Black-chins can be found at the highest parts of the park. Twenty-three individuals were counted along the Window Trail on July 19, 1969 (Wauer). There is a decrease in numbers after mid-September, but it usually can still be found along the river through December. Like the Lucifer Hummingbird, it can often be found at flowering Tree Tobacco plants. The latest sighting of any year is one by Bill Bromberg at Boquillas on December 28, 1961.

COSTA'S HUMMINGBIRD. *Calypte costae*

There are only two sightings of this little western desert species. A lone male was seen at 7,000 feet elevation on Lost

Mine Trail, August 7, 1966 (Wauer), and another male was seen perched on an Ocotillo at Rio Grande Village, December 17, 1966 (Wauer and Dick Russell).

ANNA'S HUMMINGBIRD. *Calypte anna*

Rare but regular fall migrant and irregular winter visitor. Borell first collected one in the Chisos Basin on October 23, 1936, and Lena McBee and Lovie Mae Whitaker found it at Boot Springs on July 24, 1940. There were no other sightings until 1967, when Kent Rylander and I collected an immature male near Santa Elena Canyon on November 5 (Wauer and Rylander, 1968). It has since been seen several times along the Rio Grande. It remained in the Santa Elena Canyon area throughout December, 1967; one was seen on the December 21 Christmas Bird Count. Two were found on the December 22, 1970, Christmas Count at Rio Grande Village (Wauer). Four males were found at Rio Grande Village on November 22, 1969, and an immature male was seen near the Boquillas Crossing on September 16 and 18, 1970 (Wauer). It apparently overwinters in the area some years; I found one near Boquillas Crossing on February 6, 1968.

BROAD-TAILED HUMMINGBIRD. *Selasphorus platycercus*

Common summer resident of the pinyon-juniper-oak woodlands and fairly common migrant. It has been recorded every month but January. I have found it along the river as early as February 3, 1967, and February 11, 1969, but it does not reach its nesting grounds until March 23. An adult male was seen defending a territory at Boot Springs on March 30, 1967 (Wauer), and Julie Hotchkiss and Sharon and Becky Wauer found an adult female feeding two fledged young at Laguna Meadow on May 17, 1969. There is some post-nesting movement to the lower slopes of the mountains when Century Plants begin to bloom in April and May, but the Mountain Sage blossoms become the favorite food source for all the Chisos hummers by July. A high count of twenty-six Broadtails was recorded in the vicinity of these red-flowered bushes in Boot Canyon on August 9, 1969 (Wauer).

Hummingbird numbers in the mountains drop off drastically by mid-September, when there is a general exodus throughout the park, except for the floodplain, where there is a slight increase. Feeders at Panther Junction continue to be used, however; one female Broad-tail fed there constantly until December 23, 1966. For the most part, hummingbird sightings in late September through November and as late as December 17 (Wauer) are restricted to Tree Tobacco stands along the river.

RUFOUS HUMMINGBIRD. *Selasphorus rufus*

Rare migrant in spring and common in late summer and fall. This is the first of the fall migrants to arrive in the mountains; the birds may appear there as early as July 20 and become abundant on flower-covered slopes by early August. Charles Bender counted more than fifty Rufous Hummers along the South Rim Trail on August 19, 1966. As in the case of the other mountain hummers, it prefers the Mountain Sage to Century Plants. There is a considerable decrease in numbers by mid-September, but a few can usually be found at flowering Mountain Sages until October 23. It has been recorded along the river through December 22. Springtime sightings are few: Mr. and Mrs. A. L. Rawls saw one near Burro Mesa Pouroff on February 7, 1967, and I observed one at Rio Grande Village on March 7, 1967.

ALLEN'S HUMMINGBIRD. *Selasphorus sasin*

I have recorded this hummer in the park on five occasions: at Boot Springs on August 10, 1968, and August 15, 1966, in Green Gulch on August 24, 1967, along the lower part of the Window Trail on October 5, 1970, and at Laguna Meadow on August 22, 1971. The last sighting was of an adult male in company with Brent Wauer, who was intimately familiar with this bird in California.

CALLIOPE HUMMINGBIRD. *Stellula calliope*

There is but one park record of this little hummer: a lone male found feeding on Mountain Sage at 6,500 feet elevation in upper Boot Canyon on August 7, 1969 (Wauer). It was recorded in West Texas on three occasions in 1971: Shine Bounds found two at his feeder in Alpine, Geth White saw one in El Paso in late July, and Pansy Espy saw one in Fort Davis the first week of August.

RIVOLI'S HUMMINGBIRD. *Eugenes fulgens*

Uncommon summer resident in the higher woodlands of the Chisos Mountains. It is rarely seen below 6,000 feet elevation, but Pete Koch observed one at Cattail Falls on April 28, 1967. This and the following species are the two largest of North America's hummers. The male Rivoli's has no white in the tail, as does the Blue-throat. Rivoli's Hummers prefer the somewhat higher and drier pinyon-juniper-oak localities, whereas the Blue-throat is more numerous in the moist canyons and oak zones. Although I have found no proof of nesting, the Rivoli's Hummer has been seen regularly from March 30 through August, and it has been reported for the Chisos Mountains since 1955, when Dixon found it at Boot Springs on July 21 and 26 (Dixon and Wallmo, 1956).

BLUE-THROATED HUMMINGBIRD. *Lampornis clemenciae*

Common summer resident in the high Chisos canyons, and uncommon to 5,000 feet. There also are two sightings of migrants along the river: Roy Hudson saw one at Lajitas on May 22, 1964, and I saw a lone male at Boquillas on April 11, 1969. It has been reported for the park from March 30 to September 26 and is surprisingly common in Boot Canyon during summer; I counted five pairs along a one-mile stretch on May 9, 1969, and twelve individuals there on August 9, 1969. Birds do not arrive on their nesting grounds until mid-April and depart by late September; I found only three individuals in Boot Canyon on September 19, 1970. Blue-throats utter a loud *seep* that can be heard constantly when they are present. The sharp *chip* of the Rivoli's Hummer is almost never heard.

WHITE-EARED HUMMINGBIRD. *Hylocharis leucotis*

Rare post-nesting visitor to the Chisos highlands. There is one sighting by Philip Allen and Anne LeSassier from Boot Springs on April 27, 1963. Tarleton Smith collected a female in the Chisos Mountains on July 7, 1937, which represents the first Texas record for the species. Harold Schaafsma reported it near the South Rim in July, 1953. I have found it only twice in five years—lone males feeding on Mountain Sage at 6,800 feet along the north slope below Emory Peak on July 17 and August 13, 1967.

BROAD-BILLED HUMMINGBIRD. *Cynanthus latirostris*

This is another rare visitor to the Big Bend, but apparently it nests at mesquite thickets along the river. It was first reported by Quillin (1935), who found a nest containing eggs at the Johnson Ranch on May 17, 1934. Terry Maxwell found a lone female Broad-bill feeding on Tree Tobacco flowers at Johnson Ranch on May 20, 1970. I have not found it along the river in spite of several attempts. It has also been reported twice from the Chisos Mountains. Mr. and Mrs. Leon Bishop observed it feeding on Mountain Sage along the Lost Mine Trail on October 20, 1966, and I found one in Boot Canyon on August 7, 1969.

KINGFISHERS: Family Alcedinidae

BELTED KINGFISHER. *Megaceryle alcyon*

Fairly common migrant and rare winter visitor. It has been recorded every month but June; there is an absence of records only from May 14 to July 9. I have found no evidence of nesting, but some years this bird reaches the Big Bend in early July, and individuals remain at ponds and appropriate stretches along the Rio Grande for several months. Migrants are most common along the river, but I found a lone bird at Panther Junction on April 6, 1969, and one at 6,600 feet elevation in Boot Canyon on September 28, 1969. Most sightings are of one or two individuals, but six were recorded at Rio Grande Village on October 3, 1968 (Wauer).

GREEN KINGFISHER. *Chloroceryle americana*

Sporadic post-nesting visitor at ponds and clear water along the Rio Grande from August 6 to October 27. There is also an earlier sighting in Boquillas Canyon by Terry Moore and W. J. Jones, on June 20, 1966. Apparently, this species has increased its range in recent years; there are no records prior to 1966. There were no sightings in 1967, but two individuals were recorded at Rio Grande Village from August 6 through October 27, 1968 (Wauer). A single bird was seen there several times in September, 1969, and none were recorded in 1970 or 1971.

The Ringed Kingfisher (*Megaceryle torquata*) has been seen regularly as far up the Rio Grande as Falcon Dam in recent years, and has nested since 1970. I believe it is only a matter of time before it will be recorded in the Big Bend area.

WOODPECKERS: Family Picidae
YELLOW-SHAFTED FLICKER. *Colaptes auratus*

Rare migrant and sporadic winter resident. Records range from October 15 to March 28. Except for lone birds seen at Laguna Meadow on October 22, 1967, at Dugout Wells on December 30, 1966 (Wauer), and in the Basin from March 4 to 10, 1971 (Ruth Jessen), all sightings are from the vicinity of the river floodplain. It apparently occurs sporadically in winter; I found four at Rio Grande Village almost daily in 1966–67, but found it only four times in 1967–68, never in 1968–69, and only once in 1969–70—a lone male on November 8, 1969.

RED-SHAFTED FLICKER. *Colaptes cafer*

Uncommon summer resident in the Chisos highlands, and common migrant and winter resident. Big Bend's breeding flicker is of special interest because it represents the northern breeding population of the Mexican race of Red-shafted Flicker—*Colaptes cafer nanus*—which is resident only in the Chisos Mountains in the United States. Adult birds were discovered feeding young at a nest twelve feet high in a dead Ponderosa Pine snag near Boot Springs on May 8, 1968 (Wauer). By early July, post-nesting birds disperse into lower elevations and can be found in the Basin and Green Gulch.

Flickers are most numerous in migration from late February to April 23 in spring, and September 24 through November in fall. Migrants and wintering birds can be expected anywhere, although they are most common below 5,600 feet elevation.

GOLDEN-FRONTED WOODPECKER. *Centurus aurifrons*

Rare migrant in the park, but resident at Calamity Creek, south of Alpine, where one was found carrying food to a hole high on a cottonwood on May 26, 1968 (Wauer). I have recorded it on Christmas Counts there in 1967, 1968, and 1970. Park sightings range from April 2 to May 13 in spring, and there are two fall sightings; lone birds were seen at Boquillas on September 10, 1955 (National Park Service files), and I observed one at 5,900 feet elevation on the Lost Mine Trail on November 6, 1966.

RED-HEADED WOODPECKER. *Melanerpes erythrocephalus*

There are two sightings only; Tarleton Smith observed one in the Chisos Basin on June 27, 1936, and Allan Atchison reported one from Boot Canyon on July 11, 1964.

ACORN WOODPECKER. *Melanerpes formicivorus*

Common resident in the Chisos woodlands, abundant at Boot Springs. Most numerous in the upper canyons, it does

occur to the lower edge of the oaks in late summer and fall
and has been seen a considerable distance from the Chisos
woodlands; I was surprised to find a lone bird among the
mesquites at Solis (1,950 feet) on November 11, 1967. There
are several nesting records, all in live oaks or pinyons from
early May through July. There also is a rather interesting
record of a storm-killed bird. Paul Gerrish reported that he
found a dead Acorn Woodpecker on the trail in Boot Canyon
on October 10, 1969, shortly after an extremely heavy,
fifteen-minute hailstorm had passed through the area. The
most accessible place to see this bird is within the canyon
along the north side of the Basin Campground.

LEWIS' WOODPECKER. *Asyndesmus lewis*

There are three park records of this vagrant. Sutton collected one at Boot Springs on May 1, 1935, the Woolfendens
observed one at Rio Grande Village in January, 1963, and I
found one flying south over Boot Canyon on October 22,
1968. The Clay Millers recorded it at their ranch in October,
1959, and December, 1963.

YELLOW-BELLIED SAPSUCKER. *Sphyrapicus varius*

Uncommon migrant and fairly common winter resident.
Records range from September 23 through March 29, and
there is a late sighting of a lone bird at Rio Grande Village,
following a period of stormy weather, on May 3, 1969
(Wauer). It occurs throughout the wooded parts of the park
in winter but is most easily found at areas of cottonwoods in
the lowlands, such as Rio Grande Village and Cottonwood
Campground. Migrants usually are found singly, but on
October 25, 1967, I counted twenty or more birds at Rio
Grande Village.

WILLIAMSON'S SAPSUCKER. *Sphyrapicus thyroideus*

Sporadic migrant and winter visitor. It was first reported
by Porter, who collected one in Pine Canyon on October 18,
1957. None were recorded again until the 1967–68 winter,

when it was seen on a number of occasions: Mr. and Mrs. O.
D. Moreen saw two at Rio Grande Village on October 28;
I found lone birds at the South Rim on November 5, at Laguna Meadow on November 24 and December 3, and at Boot
Springs on February 22 and 23; and Siglin saw one at Laguna Meadow on December 28. I have not seen this woodpecker in the area at any other time during my five years'
residency, although Maurice Mackey reported one on the
Lost Mine Trail, November 26, and Jim Tucker found one
at Laguna Meadow on December 29, 1970.

LADDER-BACKED WOODPECKER. *Dendrocopos scalaris*

Common resident below 6,000 feet elevation and irregular
post-nesting visitor above. This is the common woodpecker
of the Chihuahuan Desert. I have found it nesting in cottonwoods, willows, oaks, pinyon pines, Century Plant stalks,
utility poles, and wooden signposts. Totals of twenty-two,
sixteen, thirty-two, twenty-four, and thirty-four were found
on the Rio Grande Village and Chisos Mountains Christmas
Counts in 1966, 1967, 1968, 1969, and 1970, respectively.

TYRANT FLYCATCHERS: Family Tyrannidae

EASTERN KINGBIRD. *Tyrannus tyrannus*

Rare fall migrant, and one springtime record. I found one
at Dugout Wells on May 13, 1967. The few fall sightings
consist of lone birds, mostly juvenals, between August 25 and
September 16. Except for one seen at Grapevine Spring on
September 2, 1950 (Sprunt, Jr.), all fall records are from the
lowlands near the river.

TROPICAL KINGBIRD. *Tyrannus melancholicus*

Rare post-nesting visitor along the Rio Grande. During the
1971 summer I found a lone bird defending a territory and
nest-building on a cottonwood at Rio Grande Village; it remained in the area near the lake behind the store from June
22 through August 4. As far as I could determine, it remained

alone, but continued vigorously to defend a territory. I have recorded Tropical Kingbirds on a number of occasions from August 15 to September 19. A juvenal, one of three birds seen at Cottonwood Campground on September 2, 1968, was collected (Wauer) and was identified as the *couchii* form by Allan Phillips.

WESTERN KINGBIRD. *Tyrannus verticalis*

Rare summer resident, fairly common spring migrant, and uncommon in fall. It nested on cottonwoods at Panther Junction during June and July, 1968 and 1969, on a willow next to the river at Rio Grande Village in June, 1970, and on a tall cottonwood in the Rio Grande Village Campground in summer, 1971. Nest-building was found on June 22, adults were feeding young on July 13, and a fledged youngster was seen there on August 4 (Wauer). Spring migrants pass through the area from April 1 to May 27 and reach a peak from April 28 to May 17. Most sightings are from the floodplain, but this species has been seen almost everywhere below the Chisos woodlands. Fall migrants are few and far between and have been recorded as late as October 12. Most sightings are of lone birds, but family groups of three to five birds are occasionally recorded.

CASSIN'S KINGBIRD. *Tyrannus vociferans*

Rare summer resident and uncommon migrant. There is only one nesting record for the park; a nest was found on a cottonwood at Cottonwood Campground in mid-May, 1969, and a fledged bird was seen there June 7 (Wauer). This is the common breeding kingbird of northern Brewster and Jeff Davis counties. It is common along Calamity and Limpia creeks throughout the summer. Early spring migrants reach the Big Bend area as early as March 10 and have been recorded as late as May 18. Fall migrants trickle through the area from mid-July to the last of October; I found three at Panther Junction on the evening of September 29, 1970. A few individuals remained on the Sul Ross State University campus in Alpine until early November, 1969 (Wauer).

THICK-BILLED KINGBIRD. *Tyrannus crassirostris*

The first Texas record is a lone bird found in the Chisos Basin by Michel and O. R. Henderson on June 21, 1967 (Wauer, 1967e). It remained for about three hours near the sewage lagoons, where it was photographed by Henderson, and Dick Nelson and I observed it. On December 23, 1970, one was found on the mesquite flat near Boquillas Canyon (Wauer). It remained in the vicinity throughout the winter; Mrs. James Owen observed it in late February, the Hurlberts and Wauers observed it on March 20, and Easterla and Dave Snyder saw it on April 5, 1971. It was not seen again until May 25, when I found a lone bird on the floodplain at San Vicente Crossing. I cannot help but wonder if this bird will become established as a breeding species as it has near Patagonia, Arizona.

SCISSOR-TAILED FLYCATCHER. *Muscivora forficata*

Uncommon migrant below 4,000 feet elevation. Although this species is a common breeding bird in the vicinity of Marathon and to the north and east, it is migrant only within the park. Northbound birds pass through the park from March 30 to June 28, and fall migrants have been recorded from September 6 to October 18.

SULPHUR-BELLIED FLYCATCHER. *Myiodynastes luteiventris*

There is only one sighting of this species for the park. On May 11, 1969, Jim Tucker, Doug Eddleman, and I found a lone bird at Rio Grande Village. A previous report for West Texas by Pete Koch (Peterson, 1960) in the Davis Mountains is doubtful, since the bird was incubating eggs in an open nest in May, 1946. This species nests in cavities in Sycamores. It is a summer resident in mountain canyons in southern Arizona.

GREAT CRESTED FLYCATCHER. *Myiarchus crinitus*

Rare fall visitor along the river floodplain. There were no records of this eastern *Myiarchus* for the park prior to 1968, but since then I have found it regularly between August 24 and October 29. All three specimens collected (at Castolon on September 15, 1969, and at Rio Grande Village on September 16, 1970, and September 28, 1968) have been juvenals.

WIED'S CRESTED FLYCATCHER. *Myiarchus tyrannulus*

Rare migrant only, although there are a scattering of records from April 26 through September 13. There is no evidence of nesting, and I suspect that some of the old records are of the preceding species. This bird nests in the lower Rio Grande Valley and in southern New Mexico. There probably is some post-nesting visitation, but for the most part it is a migrant only. I found six individuals at Cottonwood Campground on May 26, 1968.

ASH-THROATED FLYCATCHER. *Myiarchus cinerascens*

Common summer resident, common spring migrant and uncommon in fall, and sporadic in winter. From mid-March through July 26 this is one of the most numerous birds of the Big Bend area. It nests along the river floodplain, at springs, in arroyos within the desert, and upward into the highest parts of the pinyon-juniper woodlands. By the last of July, however, summering birds leave their breeding grounds. They then become uncommon, except for occasional migrants along the river and in the desert washes. Although these birds gather in family groups after nesting in the western part of the Southwest, the majority of the fall migrants that pass through the Big Bend area until late September are alone.

Wintering birds occur rather sporadically. Two or three

individuals can sometimes be found at cottonwood and mesquite groves in the lowlands. I found this bird at Rio Grande Village and near Castolon regularly during the winters of 1966–67, 1967–68, and 1968–69, but only twice during December, January, and February, 1969–70.

OLIVACEOUS FLYCATCHER. *Myiarchus tuberculifer*

Rare migrant and post-nesting visitor. A specimen collected by Van Tyne and Sutton at Glenn Springs, June 17, 1932, represents the first for Texas. It has since been seen on a number of occasions from April 7 to July 7, and there is one late sighting of three birds at Rio Grande Village on October 23, 1968 (Wauer). The Hoffmans saw one on the Lost Mine Trail on May 18, 1957; Marshall found three in the Chisos Basin on July 8, 1962; I found one in the upper Chisos Basin on July 7, 1969, and three singing individuals in Boot Canyon on May 8 and 9, 1970, and Marjory Williams observed one on the Lost Mine Trail, May 24, 1972.

EASTERN PHOEBE. *Sayornis phoebe*

Fairly common winter resident along the river from October 8 through April 1. I have found it regularly at Rio Grande Village and Cottonwood Campground each winter.

BLACK PHOEBE. *Sayornis nigricans*

Fairly common resident along the river and a rare migrant. Nest-building was found inside the motel ruins at Hot Springs on March 26, 1969; a Say's Phoebe was building a nest not more than fifty feet away. Although the Black Phoebe can usually be found easily before nesting, it is very shy and one must often search for it during the nesting period. Soon after mid-July, however, adults and young appear everywhere along the river and at adjacent ponds. Migrants are few and far between but pass through the area from mid-March to April 11 in spring and from early August through September in fall. Sightings are all from the vicinity of the river, except for one at the Old Ranch on September 9, 1966

(Wauer), and one found by Walter Boles, Jim Shields, and John St. Julien at Boot Springs on August 10, 1970.

SAY'S PHOEBE. *Sayornis saya*

Fairly common in summer and common migrant and winter resident. Some birds are permanent residents; I have banded and recaptured birds at Panther Junction throughout the year. Breeding birds begin to nest in mid-March. In 1968, a pair nested in the deserted Daniel's house at Rio Grande Village in April and again in July; fledged birds were seen on May 10 and August 6 (Wauer). Young birds left a nest at Panther Junction on July 7, 1970. There is some post-nesting movement into the highlands, where birds can be seen up to 7,200 feet elevation. Migrants pass through the area from mid-March through mid-May in spring and during September and October in fall. Although most of the migrant Say's Phoebes pass through the lowlands, occasional birds are found in Boot Canyon, along the Lost Mine Trail, and at other highland areas. From early November through April, however, there are no sightings above 5,500 feet elevation.

YELLOW-BELLIED FLYCATCHER. *Empidonax flaviventris*

There are but two records of this eastern flycatcher. Specimens were taken in lower Pine Canyon on September 3, 1968, and at Rio Grande Village on September 1, 1969 (Wauer). Since this bird may be easily overlooked, it may be more common in fall than the two records indicate.

TRAILL'S FLYCATCHER. *Empidonax traillii*

Rare summer resident and uncommon migrant from May 11 to 28 in spring, and fairly common migrant from July 21 through September 24 in fall. Specimens were taken at Grapevine Spring on July 21, 1956 (Texas A&M), at a tank near Panther Junction on June 14, 1968 (Easterla), and at Rio Grande Village on August 25, 1967 (Wauer).

LEAST FLYCATCHER. *Empidonax minimus*

Uncommon spring migrant from April 20 to May 29, and common fall migrant from July 21 through October 10. It has been recorded at all elevations, but is most numerous in the lowlands. Specimens taken include four in September at various elevations and one in the Chisos Basin on May 3, 1967 (Wauer).

HAMMOND'S FLYCATCHER. *Empidonax hammondii*

Fairly common spring migrant from March 24 through May 17, and rare in fall from August 24 to September 20. It has been recorded at all elevations but is most numerous in the mountains. Specimens taken include one from the Chisos Basin on March 24, 1935, Laguna Meadow on May 3, 1935, Boot Canyon on May 6 and 7, 1932, Pine Canyon on May 9 and 14, 1933 (Van Tyne and Sutton), Boquillas Crossing on April 12, 1967, and Rio Grande Village on September 6, 1968 (Wauer), and September 20, 1957 (Porter).

DUSKY FLYCATCHER. *Empidonax oberholseri*

Fairly common spring migrant from April 22 through May 17, a lone fall sighting at Castolon on September 15, 1969 (Wauer), and sporadic in winter. During the first two weeks of May it may be numerous within the Chisos woodlands and rare along the river. There are several records along the floodplain during the winters of 1968–69 and 1970–71, but I did not find it other winters. Specimens taken include one in Pulliam Canyon on May 2, 1967, Laguna Meadow on May 4, 1967, Boot Springs on May 9, 1969, Green Gulch on May 16, 1968, and Santa Elena Canyon on December 30, 1968 (Wauer).

GRAY FLYCATCHER. *Empidonax wrightii*

Uncommon spring migrant from April 3 through June 6. There is a lone fall sighting of one bird at Boot Springs on August 29, 1970 (Easterla and Tucker). Most spring records are from the mountains, but I found lone birds at Rio Grande Village on April 8, 1968, April 8, 1970, and April 3, 1971. Van Tyne and Sutton reported specimens taken in the Chisos Basin on April 26 and 27, 1935, at Pine Canyon on May 1, 1933, and five in the Chisos Mountains from May 5 to 23, 1932.

WESTERN FLYCATCHER. *Empidonax difficilis*

Common only in Boot Canyon in summer and a rare migrant. Records range from April 1 through October 5. It arrives on its nesting grounds in mid-April and remains until late August. Nests are built on cliffs and overhangs along the drainage; nest-building was found on June 10, 1969, and fledged birds were seen on July 19 (Wauer). Dave Wolf found an adult feeding young at Boot Springs on August 22, 1968. Fall migrants were found in the Chisos Basin on October 4, 1968; a specimen was taken in Pine Canyon on September 7, 1955 (Texas A&M); and I found lone birds at Dugout Wells on September 11, 1967; and September 11, 1968. It has been recorded only once along the river; I observed a lone bird at Rio Grande Village on April 1, 1969.

COUES' FLYCATCHER. *Contopus pertinax*

Rare visitor to the high mountains. A specimen collected in the Davis Mountains by Austin Paul Smith (1917) on September 12, 1916, represents the first record for Texas. It has since been recorded on three occasions: Sharon Wauer and I saw one near the South Rim on September 4, 1966, and I heard one calling its very distinct *ho-say maria* song above Laguna Meadow on June 8, 1968. A search for the bird the following day was unsuccessful. On May 29, 1971, Ted Parker and Harold Morrin heard and saw one just above Juniper Flat.

WESTERN WOOD PEWEE. *Contopus sordidulus*

Common migrant only in the park, but it breeds in the Davis Mountains. Pansy Espy reported that it "nests every summer" there; she photographed a nest built in May, 1970. On June 12 and 27 and July 13, 1971, I found a lone individual vigorously singing and defending a territory within the Rio Grande Village Campground. Spring records range from very early sightings at Rio Grande Village on March 3, 1967 (the Wilsons), and near Persimmon Gap on March 15, 1971 (Wauer), followed by a lapse in sightings until April 13, when the bulk of northbound migrants reach the Big Bend. The spring movement continues through June 12 and reaches a peak from April 25 to May 18, when the bird may be found almost anywhere from the river to the top of the Chisos. Post-nesting birds may reach the park as early as July 16. Fall migrants are common from August 6 to mid-September, and the peak is followed by a trickle of southbound birds, particularly within the mountains, until October 30.

OLIVE-SIDED FLYCATCHER. *Nuttallornis borealis*

Fairly common migrant from April 4 to June 5 in spring, and from August 5 to October 4 in fall. It is most numerous in the mountains but occurs regularly along the river and over the desert as well. I counted nineteen individuals in the Chisos Mountains from May 12 to 15, 1967.

VERMILION FLYCATCHER. *Pyrocephalus rubinus*

Common summer resident, fairly common winter resident at localized areas along the river, and common migrant. Nest-building was found on cottonwoods at Rio Grande Village on three occasions: one during the second week of March, 1971; one five feet high on May 23, 1968; and one thirty-five feet high on May 10, 1968 (Wauer). I observed an adult male feeding a fledged youngster as late as August 1, 1967. It is most common as a spring migrant from March 7 through mid-April, when it may be found up to 4,000 feet elevation. Brodrick found one at Dagger Flat on March 9, 1956, and it regularly visits Panther Junction from March 7 to 25. There apparently is some post-nesting movement along the river and into the lowlands, as Dick Rasp found one at

Oak Spring on July 12, 1964. Most of the breeding birds remain on their nesting grounds until late September, however. During early October it may become rare at Rio Grande Village, but by the third week of October another wave of migrants seems to boost the population considerably. I have found it regularly at Rio Grande Village, but nowhere else within the park, during December, January, and February, except in winter 1969–70. Some winters it can be found at Cottonwood Campground as well.

LARKS: Family Alaudidae

HORNED LARK. *Eremophila alpestris*

Uncommon migrant and rare winter visitor in the park, but common all year on the open grasslands near Marathon and north to Fort Stockton. It has been reported for the park every month but July, August, and September, but I have not found it regularly anywhere. Most park observations are of small flocks of three and four birds along the River Road, on Tornillo Flat, or in the Chisos Basin.

SWALLOWS: Family Hirundinidae

VIOLET-GREEN SWALLOW. *Tachycineta thalassina*

Uncommon summer resident in the Chisos Mountains, fairly common spring migrant, and rare in fall. This species may begin to move along the Rio Grande as early as February 24 and may become regular along the river by the first of March. It does not reach its nesting grounds in the mountains until March 17. The movement of spring migrants continues along the river and occasionally over the desert until May 3. Nesting birds utilize cliffs above 5,200 feet in Green Gulch, the Basin, upper Juniper and Pine canyons, and on Emory Peak. Nesting apparently is completed and the birds move elsewhere by the second week of July;

there is a lapse of records for the park from July 7 to August 30, when southbound migrants begin to reappear along the river. The fall migration is sparse but extends through October 12. There is also a single winter sighting of two birds seen at Rio Grande Village, December 28, 1965, by Raymond Fleetwood.

TREE SWALLOW. *Iridoprocne bicolor*

Uncommon migrant along the river from March 9 to May 1 in spring, and from August 25 to September 9 in fall. It usually occurs alone or in twos or threes with other migrating swallows. It apparently is also a rare winter visitor; Adele West found it at Rio Grande Village on January 17, 1963.

BANK SWALLOW. *Riparia riparia*

Uncommon spring migrant along the river from March 10 to May 20, and there are three fall sightings. I found lone birds at Castolon on August 17 and at Rio Grande Village on August 19, 1968, and Easterla saw two at Santa Elena Canyon on August 30, 1970. Like the preceding species, it is never common but can be found with other migrating swallows at appropriate times of the year. There is also a December 8, 1967, sighting of a lone bird at Rio Grande Village (Wauer).

ROUGH-WINGED SWALLOW. *Stelgidopteryx ruficollis*

Fairly common summer resident, common spring migrant, and uncommon in fall and winter along the river. It is most numerous from mid-February through May, when northbound migrants are passing through the area and breeding birds are nesting. Two pairs of Rough-wings were seen carrying nesting materials into holes in a mud bank at Solis on February 21, 1969 (Wauer). Sightings continue throughout the summer at localized areas along the river, such as Hot Springs, Solis, and Castolon. There is only a slight increase of birds in late September as fall migrants move along the waterways. Wintering birds can usually be found in small flocks of three to a dozen individuals along the Rio Grande. Christmas Counts at Castolon and Rio Grande Village were twenty-nine, sixty-one, sixty, twenty-six, and forty-two in 1966, 1967, 1968, 1969, and 1970, respectively.

BARN SWALLOW. *Hirundo rustica*

Summer resident at a few localized places, and fairly common migrant from March 4 to late May in spring and from early August through November 5 in fall. The earliest arrival date at Panther Junction is March 24. Nesting occurs on buildings at Rio Grande Village, Castolon, and Panther Junction. Two clutches are usually produced. The first young are usually fledged by late June; young left the nest at Rio Grande Village store on June 26, 1968. A second clutch is usually produced during August; nestlings were banded at Panther Junction on September 11, 1966, and September 2, 1968. It is most numerous in migration, and flocks of fifteen to fifty birds can often be found along the river; it also has been seen over the desert and high in the Chisos Mountains.

CLIFF SWALLOW. *Petrochelidon pyrrhonota*

Common summer resident along the river and less numerous in the desert, and uncommon migrant. It arrives as early as March 20 and begins to nest immediately. Nests can be found on cliffs adjacent to the river throughout the canyons and at other appropriate places. Early birds also reach bridges and cliffs at a considerable distance from the river; several were seen nest-building in Boquillas Canyon on March 22, 1969, and twelve individuals were found at nests on the upper Tornillo Creek bridge on March 25, 1968 (Wauer). It apparently nests on cliffs in rather inhospitable places during wet years; I found several places on Tornillo Flat where Cliff Swallow nests had been constructed earlier but were not in use at the time. Philip Allen searched for Cliff Swallow nests in 1963 and reported fifty-three at the upper Tornillo Creek bridge, thirty-two at lower Tornillo Creek bridge, fifty-five at Hot Springs, eight at Alamo Creek bridge below Castolon, and twenty-one at Devil's Den.

The bulk of the nesting birds leave their first breeding grounds by mid-July, but there apparently is a second nesting some years. I found nests under the bridges at Nine Point Draw and upper Tornillo Creek occupied during August, 1970. Lone birds or small flocks of migrants can be expected along the river to mid-October, and a flock of seven birds was sighted at Hot Springs on October 20, 1967 (Wauer).

CAVE SWALLOW. *Petrochelidon fulva*

There is one small colony of these birds known to nest within the park. Don Davis first found nests of this species in the twilight part of a cave along the eastern slope of Mariscal Mountain in January, 1969. On May 27, Don and I visited this area and found a total of thirteen Cave Swallows using two caves; there were three active nests. Cliff Swallows were nesting near the entrance of one cave. On July 17, Easterla found twenty to twenty-five birds at the caves and three more active nests. Cave Swallows were found nesting there again in May and July, 1970. This species is rare in migration, but I have found it at Castolon on August 16, 1969, and April 4, 1970, and at Rio Grande Village on September 14, 1968 (twenty-five to thirty individuals), October 5, 1969, and April 18, 1970.

PURPLE MARTIN. *Progne subis*

The status of this swallow is questionable. It has been seen within the park only once in recent years: the Schaughencys saw one at Hot Springs on April 22, 1971. Van Tyne and Sutton reported a specimen taken at San Vicente on May 20, 1935; Tarleton Smith found three in lower

Green Gulch on June 11, 1935; and Sprunt, Jr., and Dick saw it at Hot Springs on July 24, 1951.

JAYS, RAVENS, and NUTCRACKERS:
Family Corvidae

BLUE JAY. *Cyanocitta cristata*

There are two records of this eastern jay for the park. Brodrick reported one at Panther Junction on November 2, 1956, and one stayed at Castolon from December 30, 1967, to February 6, 1968 (Court and Wauer).

SCRUB JAY. *Aphelocoma coerulescens*

This species is common just north of the park in the Del Norte and Davis mountains, but it is only accidental in the Chisos. I have seen it only once in the park, a lone bird in lower Green Gulch on December 28, 1967. Because it can easily be confused with the common Mexican Jay, it may be more regular during winter than this single sighting would indicate.

MEXICAN JAY. *Aphelocoma ultramarina*

Common resident above the lower limits of the pinyon-juniper-oak woodlands in the Chisos Mountains. This is one of the most conspicuous birds of the mountains and flocks of 5 to 18 are common. Christmas counters recorded 25 in 1966, 222 in 1967, 180 in 1968, 18 in 1969, and 106 in 1970. Nesting occurs during April, May, and June; nests were found on a Grave's Oak near Laguna Meadow on May 8, 1970, and on an Emory Oak near the Window on May 11, 1968 (Wauer); and Philip Allen reported fledged birds at Boot Springs on June 1, 1963. There apparently is some local movement to lower elevations during some winters. One was seen in upper Big Brushy Canyon, in the northern part of the Dead Horse Mountains, on October 13, 1969, and one was found at Rio Grande Village on December 13, 1969 (Wauer).

The Mexican Jay is the only resident jay of the Chisos and del Carmen mountains, although there are habitats suitable for Steller's and Scrub jays. It appears that the Mexican Jay is dominant wherever it occurs.

COMMON RAVEN. *Corvus corax*

Fairly common resident from the Rio Grande to the top of the Chisos Mountains. This is the common raven throughout the park; White-necks are only occasionally seen within the desert lowlands. Common Ravens nest early in spring; young were fledged from a nest on Tornillo Flat by mid-April, 1968, and adults were feeding young in a nest in lower Hot Springs Canyon on May 4, 1970 (Wauer). Post-nesting birds residing near the mountains roost in the highlands and move into the desert to feed each morning. They can often be found soaring over mountain ridges and peaks in the afternoons; forty-three birds were seen over the South Rim on May 10, 1969, and thirty-two were observed circling over Boot Canyon on October 22, 1967 (Wauer). In winter, more than forty individuals use a deep cut in the cliff near Boot Canyon Pouroff as a nightly roost.

WHITE-NECKED RAVEN. *Corvus cryptoleucus*

Rare summer visitor and migrant in the lower part of the Big Bend, but common on the mesquite flats in the northern part of Brewster County and north into New Mexico. Although this species generally is considered to be resident over most of its range, I have found it to move into the northern Big Bend area during March and April. Nests can be found on mesquites and utility poles along the highways between Marathon and Sanderson and west toward Marfa. The status of this raven apparently has changed within the park in recent years. Van Tyne and Sutton reported it as common, but I have found it only irregularly, and there are no records for December and February. Most of the recent park sightings are from Tornillo Flat and south to the lower Tornillo Creek bridge. The majority of these records are of one or two individuals, but David Simon found a flock of six on August 30, 1967.

PINYON JAY. *Gymnorhinus cyanocephala*

There is only one record of this gregarious bird for the park; Karl Haller found three individuals in the Chisos Mountains on December 24, 1950. Pansy Espy reported that thousands were found in the Davis Mountains from the last of September, 1968, until June 18, 1969. She said: "That year there was a bumper crop of Pinyon Nuts. On April 4, 1969, I sat in one spot and counted over a thousand Pinyon Jays as they covered a hillside in one enormous loosely knit flock. The Clark's Nutcracker was here, too, at the same time, but the most I saw at one time was about five hundred—from September until the last of April. I am sure both will be back when there is abundance of food that they like."

CLARK'S NUTCRACKER. *Nucifraga columbiana*

There are two records only for the Chisos Mountains. John Galley (1951) found one on the Lost Mine Trail on October 16, 1950, and Mr. and Mrs. Forrest Roulands observed five there on October 30, 1966. Espy has recorded it in the Davis Mountains every month but June, July, and August.

TITMICE, VERDINS, and BUSHTITS:
Family Paridae

BLACK-CRESTED TITMOUSE. *Parus atricristatus*

Common resident of the Chisos Mountains. Nesting occurs during April, May, and June; nest-building was found at Juniper Spring on May 1, 1932, and at Juniper Flat on May 20, 1967, and adults were seen feeding young at Boot Springs on June 11, 1967 (Wauer). Apparently, it occasionally wanders into the lowlands; I found a lone bird at Rio Grande Village that remained from November 11 to December 12, 1969.

VERDIN. *Auriparus flaviceps*

Fairly common resident in the desert lowlands up to 4,000 feet. This little bird may be difficult to find, but a search along the lowland washes and at mesquite thickets along the river is sure to produce one or more. Nesting seems to be most common in April, May, and June, but late summer nesting is not unusual. There is some post-nesting wandering; I found one individual at Laguna Meadow on October 18, 1969. This species is famous for building nests all year around; wintertime nest-building does not mean that the bird is breeding then.

BUSHTIT. *Psaltriparus minimus*

Common resident above the lower edge of the pinyon-juniper-oak woodlands. This species includes both the black-eared and the plain phases of birds that are regarded in earlier publications as two species. Studies of the bird in Mexico, Arizona, New Mexico, and the Big Bend area have proved that most of the black-eared birds are only juvenal males. Some breeding males, however, may possess the black-eared coloration; I found a black-eared bird mounting a plain bird near the Window on March 19, 1967. It is also possible to see black-eared birds feeding plain birds and vice versa. Adults have been found to lay a second clutch of eggs before the first young have left the family; thus, fledged birds may actually help feed their younger brothers and sisters. Additional information about the color phases in these birds can be obtained by reading Phillips, Marshall, and Monson (1964:111–113) and Raitt (1967); see the bibliography for publication details.

During most of the year Bushtits occur in flocks ranging from small family groups of eight to ten birds to forty-five and fifty-five individuals. Then they are easy to locate because they constantly call to one another as they move through the woodlands feeding upon insects. Their calls may be heard from as far as two hundred feet. During the nesting season they may be rather difficult to find because they are usually quiet when incubating or feeding young. Nests have been found from mid-March to early June, usually with difficulty, because they are placed in dense foliage of junipers and pines; one nest was found among mistletoe on a Drooping Juniper in Boot Canyon on May 8, 1968 (Wauer). As the season progresses there are fewer black-eared birds, although right after nesting a flock may be composed half of black-eared and half of plain birds.

NUTHATCHES: Family Sittidae

WHITE-BREASTED NUTHATCH. *Sitta carolinensis*

Fairly common resident in the upper woodlands of the Chisos Mountains. In summer it can best be found at Laguna Meadow or in Boot Canyon among stands of tall cypress or pines. There apparently is some wandering into the lowlands in the fall; one was reported in the Basin on September 1, 1950, and I found two at Rio Grande Village on September 9 to 12, 1969.

RED-BREASTED NUTHATCH. *Sitta canadensis*

Sporadic migrant and winter visitor; common some years but completely absent most years. It was first reported for the park from October 14 to December 20, 1955: John Palmer found it at Rio Grande Village on October 14, and Youse saw it at Oak Spring on October 31, November 28, and December 6, 13, and 20. The next park records were in 1966–67 when I found one at Rio Grande Village on October 29, three at Laguna Meadow on October 30, eight in Boot Canyon on November 15 and throughout the winter to April 8, and ten at Boot Springs and along the trail to the South Rim on January 28, 1967. It was absent during the next three winters, but was again seen regularly in the mountains during the winter of 1970–71. It remained at Laguna Meadow through April; Ken Prytherch saw it there on April 30.

PYGMY NUTHATCH. *Sitta pygmaea*

There is only one series of sightings of this little nuthatch for the park; it was present in Boot Canyon from January 28 to April 15, 1967. Two individuals were seen there on January 28 and 29, March 10 and 30, and April 7 and 15 (Wauer), and Russ and Marion Wilson observed three there on March 10. This seems to be another sporadic winter visitor. The nearest nesting localities are the Davis Mountains, where "they nest every year" (Espy), and Mexico's Sierra del Carmens, about fifty airline miles southeast.

CREEPERS: Family Certhiidae

BROWN CREEPER. *Certhia familiaris*

Sporadic winter visitor and migrant. Records range from October 20 through March 10. It was quite common at Rio Grande Village and less numerous in the Chisos woodlands during the 1967–68 winter. I did not see it during the following two winters, but it was present in winter 1970–71. Like the Red-breasted Nuthatch, Brown Creepers were also common during the winter of 1955–56; Youse reported it at Santa Elena Canyon on December 4 and March 4, at Oak Creek on October 31, at Coyote on February 12. and in Juniper Canyon on March 4.

WRENS: Family Troglodytidae

HOUSE WREN. *Troglodytes aedon*

Fairly common migrant and uncommon winter resident. Migrants may be found from the river floodplain to the high Chisos canyons from April 3 to May 12 in spring and from August 27 to early November in fall. Some years there appears to be a second fall movement from mid-November to early December. Wintering populations are quite stable and birds can usually be found at Boquillas Crossing, along the

Rio Grande Village Nature Trail, near Santa Elena Crossing, and along the Window Trail.

WINTER WREN. *Troglodytes troglodytes*

Rare migrant. Northbound birds have been recorded from March 2 to May 4 and can usually be detected by their very distinct song, which they sing over and over again during the early morning. Fall migrants do not reach the Big Bend area until November 10 and become most numerous from November 20 to 24; stragglers may continue to be seen through December 27. Except for one sighting at Laguna Meadow on November 15, 1966 (Wauer), all records of this tiny wren are from the vicinity of the Rio Grande.

BEWICK'S WREN. *Thryomanes bewickii*

Abundant summer resident of the Chisos woodlands and less numerous at thickets down to 4,000 feet, and fairly common migrant and winter resident. This is the most numerous summering bird of the park's pinyon-juniper-oak woodlands. In fact, its vast repertoire of songs can be very confusing. It can sound very much like a Colima Warbler, and several observations may be necessary before one is sure which song is which. Migrant Bewick's Wrens move through the area from early March through April 9 in spring and from August 27 through October in fall. Migrants and wintering birds can be expected anywhere, but from April 10 to August 27 records are above 3,500 feet elevation.

CAROLINA WREN. *Thryothorus ludovicianus*

Irregular visitor. It has been reported for the park every month. Except for one sighting at San Vicente on July 13, 1971 (Wauer), however, there are no records from June 5 through August 28. Most sightings are from the river floodplain at Boquillas Crossing and on the Rio Grande Village Nature Trail, but there also are a few sightings in the mountains. Adele Harding found one in Boot Canyon on April 16,

1962; Allen saw one at Laguna Meadow on May 28, 1963; Rose Ann Rowlett found one at Boot Springs on June 4, 1965; and Simon found one in the Basin on August 31, 1967.

CACTUS WREN. *Campylorhynchus brunneicapillum*

Common resident below the lower edge of the mountain woodlands, and rare on the Rio Grande floodplain. This large desert wren can hardly be missed, because of its loud and raucous call and conspicuous, football-sized nests. Nest-building takes place throughout the year, and almost every kind of tree, shrub, and man-made device has been used. Bill Degenhardt reported a nest built in a pair of shorts hanging on the line. My wife discovered a nest built in a fold of a sheet one time and in the pocket of my field pants another.

LONG-BILLED MARSH WREN. *Telmatodytes palustris*

Fairly common migrant and winter resident along the Rio Grande from September 11 to May 20. The bulk of the spring migrants pass through the area from mid-March to early May, but a few stragglers have been reported as late as May 20. During the peak of the northbound movement, the last week of March and the first week of April, this wren occasionally is found a considerable distance from the river; I found one at Oak Creek on March 26 and one at Panther Junction on March 30, 1968. Fall migrants are not as numerous as those in spring, and the southbound movement is over by mid-November. A high count of fifteen birds was recorded at Rio Grande Village on October 29, 1966 (Wauer). Wintering birds are locally common at such places as the silt pond and beaver pond at Rio Grande Village.

SHORT-BILLED MARSH WREN. *Cistothorus platensis*

There is only one sighting of this little wren for the park; I found a lone bird at a tule-filled seep near Boquillas Crossing on February 14, 1967. Frances Williams and the Midland Naturalists have recorded it almost every winter below the dam at Lake Balmorhea, where it apparently is a regular winter resident.

CAÑON WREN. *Catherpes mexicanus*

Common resident of rocky canyons from the Rio Grande to the top of the Chisos. This is the bird with the clear, descending song. You are almost assured of hearing it any sunny morning in Santa Elena or Boquillas canyons. Although it prefers rocky cliffs and canyons for nesting and singing, it spends considerable time foraging for food in mesquite thickets along the river and lowland washes or among the pinyon-juniper-oak woodlands. Nest-building was found just above the Wilson Ranch in Blue Creek Canyon on April 5, 1969, and adults were seen feeding young at Boquillas on May 24, 1969 (Wauer).

ROCK WREN. *Salpinctes obsoletus*

Uncommon summer resident, common migrant, and fairly common winter resident. Summertime birds may be found from the cliffs along the river to the top of Emory Peak. Rock Wrens can almost always be found at Hot Springs and on the cliffs at the lower end of the Window Trail. Van Tyne and Sutton reported a nest with five eggs at Lajitas on May 10, 1935; Henry Howe found it nesting at Grapevine Hills on July 23, 1966; and I found three fledged young on the rocky slope below Laguna Meadow on July 20, 1969. About the first week of September there is a brief spurt of migrants through the area. Some years this movement increases dramatically from mid-October until early November, when birds are numerous below 5,500 feet elevation. Many apparently remain as winter residents, but winter residents are somewhat sporadic; Chisos Mountains Christmas counters recorded 15 in 1966, 14 in 1967, 129 in 1968, 14 in 1969, and 47 in 1970. Another increase in birds is evident in mid-March, and northbound migrants continue to pass through the area until the second week of April.

MOCKINGBIRDS and THRASHERS: Family Mimidae

MOCKINGBIRD. *Mimus polyglottos*

Common summer resident and migrant, and fairly common winter resident below 5,500 feet elevation. Summertime birds frequent almost every wash and patch of vegetation from the floodplain to the lower edge of the Chisos woodlands. Nesting has been recorded from April through August, and the breeding birds are considerably darker than those in winter. A population decline begins in mid-August and continues through the fall and winter; a low is reached from February 22 to mid-March, when the wintering birds move out of the area. On March 15 to 17, however, there is a drastic change in the population when spring migrants begin to pour into the desert lowlands. This high remains until mid-June, when the first of the nesting birds begin to disperse. Some of Big Bend's Mockers are permanent residents; a bird banded at Rio Grande Village was recorded there all twelve months of the year. Breeding birds at Panther Junction do not remain in the area, although they return each March and stay until at least mid-July.

CATBIRD *Dumetella carolinensis*

There are two park records of this bird. The first is a series of sightings at Rio Grande Village from January to March, 1963: Adele West saw it several times from January 1 to 26, the Woolfendens found it in January, and the Bedells saw one and heard it singing on March 4. It was not recorded again until 1971, when I collected one at Rio Grande Village on May 7. Clay and Jody Miller reported one seen at their ranch in Jeff Davis County on October 9 and 10, 1956.

BROWN THRASHER. *Toxostoma rufum*

Uncommon migrant and winter resident. It has been recorded from October 9 through May 20. Most sightings are from the floodplain at Rio Grande Village, the Santa Elena

Canyon picnic area, and Cottonwood Campground, but I also have found it regularly in winter at the Old Ranch. Lone birds are usual, but migrants may be seen in twos and threes.

LONG-BILLED THRASHER. *Toxostoma longirostre*

There are but two sightings of this South Texas thrasher in the park. John Rowlett observed one among the cane at Rio Grande Village in mid-August, 1965; and I found a bird that I believed to be this species in lower Glenn Draw on April 17, 1968. Clay and Jody Miller recorded lone birds at their ranch in May, 1962, and October, 1964.

CURVE-BILLED THRASHER. *Toxostoma curvirostre*

Rare in summer, common migrant, and fairly common winter resident below 5,000 feet elevation. This is a species that may have decreased as a breeding bird within the park during recent years. Van Tyne and Sutton reported it to nest at Glenn Springs in May, 1932, and Brodrick found it nesting at Panther Junction in 1961. More recently, I have found it to summer only along the northern edge of the park in the vicinity of Paint Gap, and, in 1971, it nested at Panther Junction; a juvenal bird, barely able to fly, was banded there on June 6. I had seen adults throughout May for the first time in five years. Curve-billed Thrashers are fairly common on the open mesquite lands of northern Brewster County and north to Fort Stockton and Fort Davis.

Fall migrants reach the park area by late August; an immature bird seen along the Window Trail on August 27, 1968, probably was a wanderer and not a local youngster. This bird can be found almost anywhere in the lowlands from late October through May, and it arrives at Panther Junction on October 15 and remains until April 19. It is most numerous as a migrant from mid-March to May 16, and a few stragglers are recorded to June 14. Singing birds have been recorded in migration and on their wintering grounds. The earliest song I recorded was at Panther Junction on February 11, 1969. Although most migrants pass through the lowlands, there are several Basin sightings and one from Laguna Meadow on December 23, 1967 (Wauer).

CRISSAL THRASHER. *Toxostoma dorsale*

Uncommon summer and winter resident and migrant. This species appears to have increased in recent years and may be filling the niche vacated by the decreasing Curve-billed Thrasher. Crissal Thrashers nest in a rather wide zone of habitats from the acacia-mesquite-arroyo association to the Chisos chaparral, from 3,500 to 6,500 feet elevation. Van Tyne and Sutton reported it as a nesting bird at 5,200 feet in the Basin only, but recent nesting records range from Laguna Meadow, Blue Creek Canyon, along the Window Trail, to Dugout Wells, and K-Bar Ranch—all during May and June. Nest-building was found in Blue Creek Canyon on May 8, 1969 (Wauer and Parmeter), the Hotchkisses discovered a nest in a mesquite at the K-Bar the first week of May, 1970, and I observed an adult feeding three youngsters along the Window Trail on May 25, 1969.

Post-nesting birds wander into the lowlands and may be found along the river at Rio Grande Village and Castolon during the summer. It is most numerous as a migrant from mid-March to April 10 in spring, and August 22 to early November in fall. Wintering birds can usually be found among the dense mesquite thickets along the river and up into the Chisos chaparral zones. A search near Cottonwood Campground, the flats just north of the Santa Elena Canyon picnic area, and along the Window Trail, just below the sewage lagoons, can usually produce at least a few Crissal Thrashers.

SAGE THRASHER. *Oreoscoptes montanus*

Uncommon spring migrant and sporadic in fall and winter. Records range from October 2 through April 27, and there is one summer sighting of a lone bird along the Window Trail on July 24, 1964, by Dick Rasp, which may raise some question of nesting but more likely represents an injured or nonbreeding vagrant. Spring migrants are most common from March 9 to April 7, and I found lone birds at Persimmon Gap on April 21, 1970, and at Hot Springs on April 27, 1968. Fall sightings are infrequent during October, increase during early November, and usually decrease by late November. I found fifteen to twenty individuals near Adams Ranch, just northeast of the park, on October 13, 1969, and fifty or more birds on Dog Canyon Flat on December 16, 1970. It appears that Sage Thrashers move through the area in numbers and, if such food as the Tasajillo Cactus fruit is available, they may remain for several days. I have seen several birds on the flat just west of the Boquillas Canyon parking area almost every year during the first two weeks of November.

THRUSHES, BLUEBIRDS, and SOLITAIRES:
Family Turdidae

AMERICAN ROBIN. *Turdus migratorius*

Uncommon migrant and fairly common winter visitor from October 25 throughout May 21. This is the well-known Robin of gardens and woods that can be found in flocks of hundreds. The largest flocks recorded in the park are fifteen individuals that wintered at Laguna Meadow in 1966–67, forty-five along the Window Trail on December 29, 1970, and fifty-five there on March 21, 1971 (Wauer). In spite of the fact that huge flocks can often be encountered in the Del Norte and Davis mountains to the north, Robins found in the park usually are alone or in small flocks of less than a dozen birds. They may appear anywhere but rarely remain in one place for more than a week or two. Four or five birds frequent Rio Grande Village and Cottonwood Campground each winter, and a few can usually be found wintering in the lower canyons of the Chisos Mountains. There is no apparent increase in numbers during migration, but one to ten birds may appear at Hot Springs, Panther Junction, the Basin, or elsewhere. There also are two summertime records: a lone immature bird was seen near the Basin sewage lagoons on July 19, 1969, and one there on August 24, 1970 (Wauer). I found another immature bird at Laguna Meadow on September 4, 1967. All three of these youngsters were alone and very capable of flight; they assumedly were late summer wanderers only.

RUFOUS-BACKED ROBIN. *Turdus rufopalliatus*

There is only one series of sightings of this Mexican species for the park. A lone bird was discovered at Rio Grande Village on October 23, 1966. It stayed among dense mesquite and Seepwillow near the *Gambusia* pond for eight days before disappearing. Sharon Wauer and I had an excellent look at it the first day, but it became very shy and difficult to find afterward. This record represents the first for Texas, although it has been recorded near Nogales, Arizona, a number of times since 1960.

WOOD THRUSH. *Hylocichla mustelina*

Rare spring migrant. It has been recorded only during 1967 and 1969. In 1967, I found one at Rio Grande Village on April 5, another one in upper Green Gulch (5,600 feet) on April 6, and one at Dugout Wells on April 7. In 1969, I found a lone bird at Hot Springs on May 2.

HERMIT THRUSH. *Hylocichla guttata*

Common migrant and fairly common winter resident. Early fall migrants may reach the Big Bend area by September 8, but the main southward movement does not begin until late September, reaching a peak in the middle of October and decreasing to early November. Late influxes of migrants are not uncommon; many birds were recorded along the river on December 22, 1968, and more than one hundred individuals were counted along the Window Trail on January 26, 1969 (Wauer), where a few had been seen a few days earlier. Wintering birds can usually be found along the river and throughout the canyons of the Chisos Mountains. Spring migrants become evident by mid-March; there is a relatively heavy movement through the park that lasts until April 12, when sightings sharply decrease. This low is followed by a second surge of migrants from April 26 to mid-May, and stragglers have been found as late as June 10, 1969 (Wauer). I have heard it sing in migration only twice: two singing birds at Boquillas during the morning of March 25, 1967, and two or three singing birds on the ridge above Boot Springs during the very rainy morning of May 10, 1969.

SWAINSON'S THRUSH. *Hylocichla ustulata*

Uncommon migrant from May 1 to 20 in spring and from September 1 to October 21 in fall. All the park's spring records are from the mountains, but southbound birds have been recorded throughout the park.

GRAY-CHEEKED THRUSH. *Hylocichla minima*

Rare spring migrant. Mrs. Cleve Bachman found one first at Laguna Meadow on May 10, 1967. George Shier reported it twice: in Pine Canyon on March 19, 1969, and at Glenn Springs on April 17, 1970. On April 7, 1971, Easterla and Dave Snyder observed one near Santa Elena Canyon.

EASTERN BLUEBIRD. *Sialia sialis*

Uncommon and somewhat sporadic winter resident from November 19 through March; and there is one nesting record. On April 15, 18, and 23, and May 2, 1972, I observed a lone adult male feeding four spotted youngsters in the vicinity of the lake at Rio Grande Village. The youngsters were barely able to fly on April 15. Youse first found Eastern Bluebirds in the park near Santa Elena Canyon on March 24, 1956. I found it present at Rio Grande Village all of winter, 1966–67: three individuals were seen on November 24; more than forty were counted on November 26; and seven individuals were last seen there on March 18. Less than one dozen birds spent the 1967–68 winter at Rio Grande Village

from December 21 to March 9, and about two dozen birds
wintered there from December 27, 1968, through March 21,
1969; three were found in the Chisos Basin on December 23.
Only ten birds were seen at Rio Grande Village from November 22, 1969, to February 18, 1970, and about two dozen
wintered there in 1970–71. Pansy Espy has recorded this
species from December through March in the Davis Mountains.

WESTERN BLUEBIRD. *Sialia mexicana*

Rare migrant and fairly common winter visitor from October 23 through March 31, and Allen reported it at Boot
Springs on May 24, 1963. Twenty to thirty birds frequent
Boot Canyon and Laguna Meadow to the top of the Emory
Peak section of the Chisos Mountains during mild winter
days and move into the lower basins during colder days.
These birds spend considerable time soaring along the upper
ridges and pinnacles. On November 4, 1967, I found a flock
of seventeen, twelve of which were seen eating mistletoe
berries along the slope above Boot Springs. There are only
two lowlands records of this species: Brodrick saw a flock at
Panther Junction on October 23, 1959, and I found three
birds at Rio Grande Village on November 3, 1969. Western
Bluebirds nest in the Davis and del Carmen mountains.

MOUNTAIN BLUEBIRD. *Sialia currucoides*

Rare spring migrant and uncommon and somewhat sporadic winter visitor. There are scattered springtime records
between March 14 and May 9. Van Tyne and Sutton reported specimens from Castolon on May 6, 1935, and a male
seen at 6,000 feet in Pine Canyon on May 9, 1933; more recently, twenty birds were seen at Rio Grande Village, March
14 to 24, 1970 (Wauer). Winter records range from November 5 through December, with one sighting in the Chisos Basin on February 2, 1967 (Wauer). I found a high count of
sixty to seventy-five birds on a grassy flat near San Vicente
on November 11, 1967. Some winters this species is abundant

within the open valleys of the Del Norte and Davis mountains.

TOWNSEND'S SOLITAIRE. *Myadestes townsendi*

Fairly common migrant and winter resident in the higher parts of the Chisos Mountains. The first of the fall migrants reach the area about October 11, and the southbound movement continues until late November. Several birds were found eating berries from Texas Madrones along the Emory Peak ridge on November 15, 1966 (Wauer). Wintertime residents are never numerous but can usually be found at preferred localities—along the lower Window Trail, along the north slope of Emory Peak, and in lower Boot Canyon. Spring migrants pass through the Big Bend from the last of March to mid-April, and there is a second movement from late April to May 15. There also is a June 10, 1956, sighting from the South Rim (National Park Service files).

GNATCATCHERS and KINGLETS: Family Sylviidae

BLUE-GRAY GNATCATCHER. *Polioptila caerulea*

Common summer resident, fairly common migrant, and uncommon and sporadic in winter. Spring migrants reach the park by March 8 (one at Rio Grande Village in 1969), and the northbound movement continues through April 12. Breeding Blue-grays are restricted to the mountain woodlands, and nesting is underway by late March; I found three nests under construction in Boot Canyon on March 30, 1967. Summer birds remain on their breeding grounds until about August 21, when they begin to move out of the area. Northbound birds reach the park at about the same time, and the fall migration continues through October 20. Wintering birds are somewhat sporadic in occurrence; three to five individuals were located on each of the Chisos Mountains Christmas Counts, except in 1969, when none were found.

During migration, when both species of gnatcatchers may be found together in the lowlands, they may be difficult to separate. Black-tails do not always have a tail with solid black underparts, and Blue-grays often show considerable darkness in their tail underparts. Their calls are very distinctive, however, and they can usually be aroused enough by squeaking and hissing to make them call. Black-tail calls are sharper and buzzing; those of Blue-grays are more wheezy or plaintive.

BLACK-TAILED GNATCATCHER. *Polioptila melanura*

Common resident in the shrub desert below 3,500 feet and rare to 4,000 feet elevation. Nesting occurs from March through June; the Deusings found a nest with one egg on an Allthorn at Dugout Wells on May 17, 1967; I found a nest, containing two gnatcatcher eggs and a single Brown-headed Cowbird egg, on a mesquite at Nine Point Draw on June 6, 1969. Prior to nesting, the bird is very vociferous, but it becomes quiet and sometimes difficult to find during nesting. As soon as the young are fledged, it is again easy to detect its whereabouts by its constant loud buzzing call. Although it is considered to be resident, there is an obvious decrease of birds during November and an increase in mid-February. A search among the open mesquite flats along the river from Boquillas to Santa Elena canyons and along the lower desert washes will always disclose at least a few of these little desert birds.

GOLDEN-CROWNED KINGLET. *Regulus satrapa*

Sporadic migrant and winter visitor from October 20 to February 25. There is a late sighting at Boot Springs on March 31, 1968 (Wauer). A few birds can usually be found among the floodplain vegetation below Santa Elena Canyon almost any winter, but its occurrence elsewhere is very sporadic. During the winters of 1966–67 and 1967–68, I found it regularly in the high Chisos woodlands; a high count of twenty birds was found along the trail from Boot Springs to the South Rim on January 28, 1967 (Wauer). Except for two individuals seen in the Basin on October 20, 1969, I have not seen it in the mountains since.

RUBY-CROWNED KINGLET. *Regulus calendula*

Abundant migrant and winter resident. This can be the most commonly seen bird on the river floodplain and in the higher parts of the mountains from early October through the first week of May. It has been reported as early as September 15 and as late as May 20.

PIPITS: Family Motacillidae

WATER PIPIT. *Anthus spinoletta*

Fairly common migrant and winter visitor. Fall migrants may arrive as early as September 24 but are more common from mid-October to late November. Spring migrants are most numerous from mid-March through May 11, and stragglers continue to pass through the area until May 28. Most records are from the river and creeks, but this bird may be found in the mountains as well; there are several sightings from the Basin, and I found lone birds at Boot Springs on May 8, 1968, and at Laguna Meadow on May 10, 1969. Flocks of eight to twenty birds are common, but a flock of seventy-five birds was seen along the River Road near San Vicente on November 11, 1967 (Wauer). Wintering birds are almost totally confined to the river and adjacent grassy flats, although they occasionally visit upper Tornillo and Terlingua creeks.

SPRAGUE'S PIPIT. *Anthus spragueii*

Rare migrant from April 24 to May 6 in spring and from October 18 to December 16 in fall. This buffy ground dweller prefers grassy fields and stays away from open places more than the preceding species. A walk through grassy flats in late October may frighten out one or more of these very shy birds. When frightened, Water Pipits will usually fly some distance in a flock before alighting and walking about. The Sprague's Pipit will suddenly fly out from the protection of a clump of grass, almost at your feet, fly up into the air, usually alone rather than with a flock, and then alight and hide among grass clumps. Its characteristic flight and distinctive chip readily separate this species from the more common Water Pipit.

WAXWINGS: Family Bombycillidae

CEDAR WAXWING. *Bombycilla cedrorum*

Uncommon migrant and winter visitor, but sporadic along the river in spring. There are only a few fall sightings: I found it at Panther Junction on October 12, 1970, and October 29, 1957, and at Laguna Meadow on November 4, 1967; Doug Evans saw it at Boot Springs on November 15, 1963. From late November until mid-March, it is an occasional visitor along the river, at lowland springs, and in the lower mountains. A small flock of 10 to 25 birds may remain at a particularly good feeding area for a few hours to a few days and then move on. Several of the introduced shrubs at areas of human occupation seem to be preferred by these gregarious birds. Some years, during the last half of March, Cedar Waxwings become numerous along the river, and flocks of a dozen to 200 birds can be found. A flock of 180 to 200 individuals was seen daily at Rio Grande Village from April 25 to May 19, 1969. A few remained there through May 27.

SILKY FLYCATCHERS: Family Ptilogonatidae

PHAINOPEPLA. *Phainopepla nitens*

Rare in summer and uncommon migrant and winter resident. The status of this species is uncertain. Apparently, it does nest within the area some years; Koch found a nest in lower Green Gulch in 1947, and I found a pair of birds courting in Big Brushy Canyon, south of the Black Gap Wildlife Management Area, on May 22, 1970. Sightings of one or a few birds in June and early July, such as a male and two females seen flying south over the Rio Grande Village area on July 3, 1970 (Wauer), are probably post-nesting individuals. Southbound migrants occur in small flocks along the river and in lower canyons of the Chisos during September and October. By November it seems to remain at localized areas for longer periods of time; for example, two birds were seen near Nine Point Draw four times from November 10 to 21, 1967 (Wauer). Wintering birds are irregular in occurrence, but have been reported most often from lower Green Gulch and just west of the Basin Campground. There is a slight increase in numbers in early March, and this apparent northbound movement continues through mid-April; Crabtree reported "several" individuals along the Dodson Trail and on Mesa de Anguila, April 7 to 10, 1971. This increase is followed by another lapse of records and another increase in sightings from late April to May 28.

SHRIKES: Family Laniidae

LOGGERHEAD SHRIKE. *Lanius ludovicianus*

Uncommon summer resident, and common migrant and winter resident. Nesting occurs during April, May, and June within the Sotol-grasslands and yucca zones of the park. A nest found May 28, 1968, on a Torrey Yucca at 3,000 feet elevation near Dugout Wells contained four eggs (Wauer). This bird is very shy during the nesting season and is rarely seen then, but it is more easily found after late July, when post-nesting visitors and early migrants begin to move into the lowlands. This high population decreases somewhat by November, but wintering birds remain common below 4,500 feet.

STARLINGS: Family Sturnidae

STARLING. *Sturnus vulgaris*

This exotic species has only recently begun to visit the Big Bend Park area. The first park record is a lone bird seen at Rio Grande Village in January, 1965 (Bedells). I found one there with several Brewer's Blackbirds on April 28, 1967, and three Starlings on both October 31 and December 10. Lone birds were found at Rio Grande Village on May 6 and 8, 1968, and at Cottonwood Campground on December 22, 1969 (Wauer). This species occurs at Marathon and Alpine and in time will undoubtedly become more regular in the park.

VIREOS: Family Vireonidae

BLACK-CAPPED VIREO. *Vireo atricapilla*

Summer resident at localized areas only. This little vireo was reported within the park only three times before 1966: Youse found one in upper Blue Creek Canyon on May 20, 1956, Strickling saw two at Kibby Spring on May 13, 1962, and Ben and Joan Trimble and Malcom Jenkins reported two along the Window Trail on August 15, 1963. On May 5, 1966, Jon Barlow found it nesting in Campground Canyon on the south slope of Pulliam Ridge. Since then it has been seen in this and adjacent canyons every year from May 5 through July 13. I found a nest with three eggs there on May 18, 1967, and Wolf found three pairs in these canyons on May 9, 1969. It may nest elsewhere within the Chisos Mountains, but there are no other records, although it has been seen a number of times in Blue Creek Canyon. There appears to be some post-nesting wandering; I found a juvenal within a heavily wooded area below Emory Peak at 6,100 feet on August 7, 1969. The latest sighting is one along the Window Trail on August 15, 1967 (Wauer).

WHITE-EYED VIREO. *Vireo griseus*

There are but two records of this eastern vireo for the park. The Walstons first reported one at Rio Grande Village on March 16 to 31, 1965, and Newell reported one at Hot Springs on April 9, 1969.

HUTTON'S VIREO. *Vireo huttoni*

Fairly common summer and uncommon winter resident within the Chisos woodlands. Nesting takes place during April, May, and June: a nest was found in a clump of mistletoe on an oak at Laguna Meadow on April 29, 1935 (Van Tyne and Sutton), nest-building was found there on May 17, 1969, and an adult was seen feeding a fledged bird at Boot Springs on June 9, 1968 (Wauer). Nesting birds are generally restricted to the upper parts of the woodlands, above 5,800 feet elevation. Eleven singing birds were counted between the upper Basin and Laguna Meadow on March 30, 1968 (Wauer). Its loud *sweeet* call can usually be heard for more than one hundred feet, and a few loud squeaks or hisses in the proper habitat can usually attract one or two birds. Soon after nesting, it moves into lower canyons, where it may remain throughout the winter; it can often be found in oak groves, such as those along the lower end of the Window Trail and near the east side of Panther Pass. Hutton's Vireos may wander below the woodlands on occasions; I found two individuals about three hundred feet below the pinyon-junipers in Blue Creek Canyon on February 1, 1969.

BELL'S VIREO. *Vireo bellii*

Abundant summer resident along the Rio Grande floodplain, and less numerous in summer at suitable places, such as Dugout Wells, the Old Ranch, Oak Creek, and similar thickets up to 4,500 feet elevation. Records range from March 8 through September 29. Early spring arrivals and late fall birds are quiet except for very early morning singing. By March 24 their song is one of the most commonly heard along the floodplain. Nesting occurs from April through June: I found a fledged bird at Rio Grande Village on May 10, 1968, a nest with young at Oak Creek on May 14, 1967, and an active nest located twelve feet high in a cottonwood at Castolon on June 7, 1969. Most of the summering birds move out of the area by the second week of September, but an occasional individual can usually be found for another couple of weeks.

GRAY VIREO. *Vireo vicinior*

Fairly common summer resident at suitable localities, and rare migrant and winter resident. Males arrive on their breeding grounds as early as March 17, and can easily be detected by their very distinct three-whistle song. Males vigorously defend their territories throughout the breeding period and are one of the park's most vociferous species at that time. Six singing birds were found in Blue Creek Canyon on May 8, 1969; from about one mile above the ranch house, territorial birds were found approximately every quarter of a mile. A more accessible breeding habitat lies directly across Oak Creek Canyon from the Basin Campground. Most of the canyons along the south slope of Pulliam Ridge contain one or two breeding pairs of Gray Vireos from late April through early June. Jon Barlow studied the Gray Vireo in these canyons during the summers of 1966 and 1967. There is some post-nesting dispersal: I found lone birds at Panther Junction on June 18, 1967, on the Lost Mine Trail on July 23, 1967, and in Panther Canyon on August 23, 1970. Patty Easterla found one at Panther Junction on June 6, 1971. Records of migrants are scarce; I found singing males in the center of Boquillas Canyon on March 22, 1968, and at Dugout Wells on October 8, 1968. Winter sightings are few: Karl Haller first reported one in the Chisos Basin on December 24, 1950, and Jon Barlow and I recorded it near the Chimneys and at Robber's Roost on December 30, 1970, and January 3, 1971 (Barlow and Wauer, 1971).

YELLOW-THROATED VIREO. *Vireo flavifrons*

There are three records of this large, eastern vireo: Barlow saw one just above the cottages in the Chisos Basin on May 13, 1967; I observed one foraging among the pines with several Townsend's and Orange-crowned warblers in upper Boot Canyon, September 29, 1969; and the Clay Millers found one at their ranch on May 3, 1965.

SOLITARY VIREO. *Vireo solitarius*

Rare in summer and fairly common migrant. It appears that this species nests in Boot Canyon only during wet years. A pair was found courting at Boot Springs on May 12, 1968; none were seen in the summer of 1969, but a male was found defending a territory at Boot Springs on May 7, 8, and 9, 1970 (Wauer). The spring of 1971 was very dry, and I did not find this bird in Boot Canyon. I did find a pair in upper Campground Canyon on June 16, however. Barlow found it to be a fairly common nesting bird in Madera Canyon in the Davis Mountains during May and June, 1968. It is most numerous as a migrant; as such it can be found from the river floodplain to the highest parts of the Chisos Mountains. It may appear as early as February 24; Van Tyne and Sutton reported one in Green Gulch in 1935. In recent years I have recorded it regularly after March 11; a peak is reached April 1 through 11, when the majority of the birds are of the small, yellow-green *cassinii* race. There is a paucity of sightings from April 12 to 21, followed by another heavy movement that lasts until May 17, peaking between May 2 and 9. The majority of these latter birds are the larger and lighter *plumbeous* race. Fall migrants may reach the park area as early as August 15 but are most numerous from September 8 to 25; stragglers continue to pass through the area until mid-December. I found lone birds at Laguna Meadow on November 5, 1968, in the Basin on November 24, 1968, and on the Lost Mine Trail on December 16, 1966. The majority of the fall migrants are large and light, but an occasional yellow-green bird is found. There also is a lone winter sighting by Gordon and Pat Munson at Rio Grande Village on January 20, 1971.

YELLOW-GREEN VIREO. *Vireo flavoviridis*

There is one record of this southern species for the park. Easterla collected a singing male at Cottonwood Campground on July 13, 1972. This specimen represents the first record for West Texas.

RED-EYED VIREO. *Vireo olivaceus*

Rare spring visitor from April 19 to May 17. It was first reported by Clarence Cottam at Dugout Wells on August 19, 1966. I found one there on April 28, 1967, and several were present along the river floodplain between Boquillas and Rio Grande Village from May 4 to 17, 1970. Two were caught in a mist net and banded at Rio Grande Village on May 10 and 17.

PHILADELPHIA VIREO. *Vireo philadelphicus*

Rare migrant. The Walstons reported it first at the Santa Elena Canyon picnic area on March 30, 1965. The Wards found one at Burro Spring on March 4, 1969; a lone bird was collected at Rio Grande Village on October 6, 1970 (Wauer); and the Wilsons and I found one at Cottonwood Campground on October 24, 1970. Pansy Espy reported two observations from the Davis Mountains; she and Lou C. Evans saw one in Aguja Canyon on October 19, 1968, and she found one there in April, 1969.

WARBLING VIREO. *Vireo gilvus*

Rare in summer and uncommon in migration. The summering status of this vireo is similar to that of the Solitary Vireo. It nests in the high Chisos canyons during wet years only; a pair of Warbling Vireos was seen at Boot Springs on May 3 and 14 and June 11, 1967, and a nest was found among the foliage of a Grave's Oak at Boot Springs on June

8, 1968 (Wauer). It is most numerous in migration from April 23 to May 20, when it can be found along the river or at oak groves in the mountains. Fall migrants, not as numerous, have been recorded from August 1 through September 23. There are three sightings in October and November as well: one at Rio Grande Village on October 12, 1969, in Green Gulch on October 23, 1966, and at Castolon on November 5, 1968 (Wauer).

WOOD WARBLERS: Family Parulidae

BLACK-AND-WHITE WARBLER. *Mniotilta varia*

Uncommon migrant, and there is one winter sighting by Raymond Fleetwood at Rio Grande Village on December 29, 1965. Spring migrants have been recorded in the lowlands from March 20 through May 15, but it has not been recorded in the mountains until late April. Southbound birds may arrive quite early; I found two at Rio Grande Village on July 19, 1967. There are no August records, but I have recorded it regularly from September 2 through October 5. Doug Evans observed one at Panther Junction on October 21, 1963, and Wolf saw one in Santa Elena Canyon on November 27, 1966.

PROTHONOTARY WARBLER. *Protonotaria citrea*

There is one park record of this bird: Forrest and Aline Romero photographed one in the Basin Campground on April 27, 1971. In spite of the strange location in which this bird was found, the photograph is that of an adult Prothonotary Warbler. The bird has been recorded on three occasions in the Davis Mountains: Espy found it on May 7, 1964, she and the Millers observed one on May 20, 1965, and she found another one on May 3, 1967.

WORM-EATING WARBLER. *Helmitheros vermivorus*

Rare spring migrant from April 12 through May 21. This

bird appears to be a regular spring visitor to West Texas. The first park record is that of a lone, singing bird taken from the oaks in upper Boot Canyon on May 4, 1967 (Wauer). There are several additional records from Rio Grande Village. The Harwoods found one on April 12, 1970, and I saw it there on May 1 and 6, 1969, May 5, 1970, and a singing bird on May 21, 1968. Jody and Clay Miller reported an earlier sighting at the ranch in Jeff Davis County on April 30, 1965.

GOLDEN-WINGED WARBLER. *Vermivora chrysoptera*

There is a single sighting of this little eastern warbler; Charles Crabtree and I found one among the oaks in Boot Canyon on May 9, 1970.

BLUE-WINGED WARBLER. *Vermivora pinus*

There are three records of this bird, all on the nature trail at Rio Grande Village. Adele Harding first saw one there on April 28, 1966, I found one there on May 11, 1970, and the Schaughencys saw one on April 24, 1971.

ORANGE-CROWNED WARBLER. *Vermivora celata*

Fairly common migrant and winter resident. Spring migrants begin to move through the Big Bend Country the second week of March, reach a peak from March 24 to April 11, and gradually decrease in numbers through April to May 13. Southbound migrants have been recorded as early as August 12, and a peak is reached from October 18 to November 5. There are a few instances when small flocks were recorded; for example, I found eight birds at Rio Grande Village on September 5, 1969. Wintering Orange-crowns are fairly common until early January, when there is a noticeable decrease in numbers. This population low continues until the first of the spring migrants put in their appearance.

NASHVILLE WARBLER. *Vermivora ruficapilla*

Fairly common migrant. It has been recorded from March

23 to May 15 in spring and from August 24 to October 24 in fall. This is one of the earliest of the spring warblers and is a good indicator that spring migration has started. Although it is never abundant, small flocks of three to ten birds can often be found at all elevations throughout the period of migration.

VIRGINIA'S WARBLER. *Vermivora virginiae*

Uncommon migrant in spring and rare in fall. Northbound migrants have been recorded from April 22 through May 24. Most sightings are from the mountains, but it also has been recorded along the river. At Rio Grande Village I found one on May 1, 1969, two on May 20, 1967, and one on May 24, 1967; at Santa Elena Canyon picnic area, I found one on May 1, 1967. Fall sightings include six birds found in the oaks at 4,400 feet in Panther Canyon on August 23, 1970, one at Rio Grande Village on September 6, 1968, and two at Cottonwood Campground on September 15, 1969 (Wauer). Highland birds may be confused with the more numerous Colima Warbler.

COLIMA WARBLER. *Vermivora crissalis*

Common summer resident in Boot Canyon and less numerous at a few other localities in the upper canyons of the Chisos Mountains. This probably is Big Bend's most famous bird. It is found nowhere else in the United States, and it winters in relatively inaccessible mountainous areas in southwestern Mexico. I have recorded it in Boot Canyon as early as April 10, when a lone bird was attracted by my squeaks in 1971.

During April, May, and June there is no problem finding Colimas at the proper habitat. They are very vociferous; males sing throughout the day prior to nesting but only in the early morning and on a few occasions during the day while nesting. Nests are located on the ground among leaf litter or under clumps of grass. Both adults build the nest, incubate the eggs, and care for the young. I have banded nestlings ready to leave the nest from May 25 to July 6. Very little attention is given the young after a few days of their leaving the nest. By late June the Colima may be more difficult to find. By searching among the oaks in the proper localities, however, one will usually find at least a few individuals. If a birder enters an oak grove and remains for several minutes, he will often find Colimas beginning to move about among the heavier foliage of the oaks and adjacent broadleaf trees and shrubs.

Post-nesting birds remain on their breeding grounds until mid-July, when there is a noticeable decrease in Colimas. However, they can usually be found in Boot Canyon throughout August and early September; the latest sighting is September 19. The best place in the park to find this bird consistently is along the trail in Boot Canyon just above the cabin at Boot Springs.

The Colima also occurs at a number of other localities within the Chisos Mountains. Annual counts were taken during the second week of May in 1967, 1968, 1969, and 1970. All locations where suitable habitats exist were searched. Totals of 92 Colima Warblers were found in 1967, 130 in 1968, 166 in 1969, and 118 in 1970. In all instances it was associated with oak pinyon-juniper or oak-maple-Arizona Cypress environments. Approximately 85 percent of the birds counted were located along a narrow and relatively humid canyon, with considerable overstory of vegetation, and 15 percent were located on relatively open slopes or ridges. Some localities appear to offer quite stable habitats, whereas others vary considerably. All the Boot Canyon drainages were heavily used every year, but considerable variation of populations occurs in fringe areas like Laguna Meadow and its canyons, Emory Peak, and upper Pine Canyon. In general, the distribution of breeding birds appears to be determined by the precipitation during the months just prior to the nesting season. During wet spring months, as in 1968, Colimas were found nesting along the trail just below Laguna Meadow and in upper Pine

Canyon. During dry years, such as 1969, more were found in the higher canyons and fewer in such lower and drier canyons as Pine Canyon and below Laguna Meadow.

LUCY'S WARBLER. *Vermivora luciae*

There are only a few records of this little western warbler. A singing male was seen by Noberto Ortega and me among the mesquites at Rio Grande Village on April 8, 1970. I collected a singing male at Boquillas on April 17 and found two more individuals at Rio Grande Village on May 3, 1970. In spite of searching this same area on several days afterwards, I was unable to find it again. In 1972, I found lone singing birds at Rio Grande Village on April 4 and 23. Since this habitat seems to be identical to that used by nesting birds in Arizona and New Mexico, it is possible that it may become established sometime in the future, if it does not already nest in some of the out-of-the-way mesquite thickets along the floodplain. Steve West informed me that this bird has nested near El Paso.

PARULA WARBLER. *Parula americana*

Rare summer and winter visitor and uncommon migrant. This is another bird that apparently has increased its range in recent years; there were no park records prior to 1967, but I have seen it several times since. It was first observed at Boquillas on April 7, 1967 (Wauer). In the spring of 1968 a pair was seen at the Old Ranch on April 15 (Black and Ribble), and I found one at Rio Grande Village on May 21. On November 23 one of three birds seen with a flock of several Audubon's Warblers was collected there, and on December 30 one was seen at Cottonwood Campground. In 1969 I found singing birds at Rio Grande Village on June 28 and July 1, but no indication of nesting. Lone birds were seen at Rio Grande Village on August 22 and September 5 and at Castolon on September 15. The spring of 1970 produced even more sightings; lone birds were seen at Rio Grande Village on

April 1 and 5, and three singing males found at Boquillas
Crossing on April 10 apparently stayed in the area, because
four singing Parulas were recorded there on April 17 and
two on May 3, 4, and 6. But once again I could find no evidence of nesting. In 1971, one was reported from Dugout
Wells on April 30, 1971 (Prytherch and Smith).

OLIVE WARBLER. *Peucedramus taeniatus*

There are only two records of this high-country bird for
the park. Charles Bender and William Mealy found one near
the South Rim on August 19, 1966, and I saw a lone bird in
Boot Canyon on September 19, 1970. This species nests fifty
miles to the southeast in the del Carmen Mountains of Coahuila, Mexico, and post-nesting birds can be expected.

YELLOW WARBLER. *Dendroica petechia*

Fairly common migrant, formerly a common nesting species along the Rio Grande. Van Tyne and Sutton reported
that it nested at Boquillas, Hot Springs, and San Vicente during the 1930's, but I have searched the floodplain for nesting
birds without success. In five years (1966–1971) I have
found only three summertime birds: lone males at Rio Grande Village on June 18, 1967, and July 30, 1970, and at Boquillas Crossing on July 15, 1967. Allan Phillips (1964) believes
that nesting Yellow Warblers have been extirpated by para-
sitism of Brown-headed Cowbirds in some parts of southern
Arizona, and this may well be the case in the Big Bend; cowbirds have increased in recent years and are now abundant
along the river floodplain where Yellow Warblers once nested.

Spring migrants pass through the area from April 15 to
June 18; five were found at Rio Grande Village on April 26,
fifteen on May 4, more than twenty on May 17, and none
were found on May 19, 1970. Fall migrants are less numerous and pass through the park from August 11 to September 15.

MAGNOLIA WARBLER. *Dendroica magnolia*

There are but two sightings of this bird for the park. On May 18, 1969, I watched a lone male foraging among the leaves of a walnut tree at the Old Ranch. On October 29, 1971, Stoney Burdick and I observed one at Rio Grande Village.

BLACK-THROATED BLUE WARBLER. *Dendroica caerulescens*

There are two park records. A lone male was seen and heard singing on the Rio Grande Village Nature Trail on May 11, 1969. It remained in the area for about two hours and was observed by James Tucker, Warren and Bobby Pulich, Mike Parmeter, Dave Wolf, Doug Eddleman, Betty and Charles Crabtree, and me. On the morning of June 22, 1971, Patty Easterla found a dead female bird under a window of a house at Panther Junction; the previous night had been very stormy. Pansy Espy has recorded it on two other occasions; she and the Clay Millers found one at the Miller Ranch on May 7, 1964, and Pansy observed another one in Limpia Canyon, Davis Mountains, in June, 1970.

MYRTLE WARBLER. *Dendroica coronata*

Fairly common migrant in spring and rare in fall, and uncommon winter resident. Park records range from October 18 through May 13. October and November birds are few and far between, but there is a slight increase in December. Wintering birds usually can be found along the river with its more common western "cousin," the Audubon's Warbler. There are but two winter records elsewhere: Youse found one at the Old Ranch on February 12, 1965, and I saw one in the Basin on December 22, 1967. Myrtle Warblers begin to increase slightly toward the last of February, and by mid-March this bird is as numerous in the lowlands as the Audubon's Warbler. A peak is reached in early April, but stragglers continue to pass through the park until mid-May.

AUDUBON'S WARBLER. *Dendroica auduboni*

Common migrant and winter resident from September 5 through May 27. Except for about two weeks during the first of April, this is the common bird of the "Myrtebon" complex. Recent studies by Hubbard (1969) indicate that this and the preceding bird are one species. They are regarded as two species here, however, because they can be separated by field characteristics. Typical male Audubon's have yellow throats and a large, white wing-patch, whereas typical male Myrtle Warblers have white throats and two distinct white wing-bars. This coloration is rather vague in winter birds and females, but there is still another good method of separating these two birds; the rear of the black cheek-patch turns up in the Myrtle but joins the dark on the chest or throat in the Audubon's Warbler.

This western warbler is most numerous as a spring migrant from late March through mid-May. There are several late May records as well, and D. R. Love saw one at Boquillas on June 5, 1962. Allen reported seeing 40 birds at Boot Springs on April 27, 1963, and I counted 58 along the canyon on May 12, 1967; only one was seen at Rio Grande Village on May 24, 1967. Fall migrants do not seem to be as numerous throughout the park as spring migrants, but larger flocks or "waves" have been recorded in fall. On August 30, 1966, I found 150 or more individuals with several Ruby-crowned Kinglets, Townsend's Warblers, and White-breasted Nuthatches at Laguna Meadow. On September 25, 1966, I recorded a "wave of birds near the East Rim at 8:30 A.M., including 35 to 40 Audubon's Warblers, and many Townsend's Warblers with a few Hermit Thrushes, Hepatic Tanagers, Ruby-crowned Kinglets, and Vesper Sparrows." Early fall sightings are all in the mountains, and the earliest sighting along the river is of 3 birds on September 5, 1969. The fall movement subsides by early November, but birds remain common along the river and uncommon above 4,500 feet elevation for the first half of the winter, or until the first good series of northers reach the Big Bend. Afterward it is almost impossible to find this bird in the mountains until the first of the spring migrants begin to move into the area in late March.

BLACK-THROATED GRAY WARBLER. *Dendroica nigrescens*

Rare migrant in spring and uncommon in fall, and there is one winter record. At least one bird was seen at Rio Grande Village on a number of occasions from January 1 through February 3, 1965: Dingus saw it on January 1, the Bedells reported it throughout January, and the Isleibs found it there on February 3. There are but two spring sightings of this western warbler; Youse found one at Santa Elena Canyon on April 2, 1955, and I saw a lone male at Boquillas Crossing on March 31, 1967. Fall records are more numerous and range from August 3 through October 4 in the mountains and along the river. Most sightings are of lone birds, but I found four at Laguna Meadow on August 30, 1970.

TOWNSEND'S WARBLER. *Dendroica townsendi*

Fairly common migrant and sporadic winter resident. Spring migrants move through the park area from early April through May 12. A peak is reached from May 1 to 10, when the Townsend's can be found in numbers at all elevations, although it is most numerous in the mountain woodlands. On May 8, 1967, several were heard singing on the hillside above Boot Springs, but I could not find a single bird the following morning. Fall migrants reach the park as early as August 8 but do not become numerous until the last of the month and on through mid-September; stragglers continue to pass through the area until mid-November. The high fall count was twenty-eight individuals found along the trail between the Basin Trailhead and the South Rim on September 4, 1966 (Wauer). Wintering birds occur sporadically. I have found this species regularly from December through February every year except in winter 1969–70, when none were recorded. Most wintertime sightings are from Laguna Meadow and near Boot Springs.

BLACK-THROATED GREEN WARBLER. *Dendroica virens*

Rare migrant. It was first seen with three Audubon's Warblers at the South Rim at dusk on May 12, 1967 (Wauer). Bobby Pulich next saw and heard one singing in lower Boot Canyon on May 9, 1969, and I collected a lone bird in upper Boot Canyon on August 8, 1969. The Schaughencys reported an additional sighting of one bird in Green Gulch on May 13, 1970.

HERMIT WARBLER. *Dendroica occidentalis*

Uncommon migrant from April 26 to May 14 in spring and from August 5 to September 28 in fall. A specimen taken in the Basin on May 3, 1935 (Van Tyne and Sutton), was the first for Texas. It has since been reported a number of times. Three were seen near Laguna Meadow by Robert C. Stein on May 4, 1961; Ann LeSassier found it at Boot Spring on April 26, 1963; and I observed lone birds near Laguna Meadow on April 26, 1972, and at Boot Springs on April 28, 1967, and May 9, 1968. Fall records include a specimen in upper Boot Canyon on August 8, 1969, one seen at Rio Grande Village on August 28, 1969, lone birds at Boot Springs on August 29, 1970, and September 28, 1969, at Laguna Meadow on August 30, 1970, and in the Basin on August 31, 1966 (Wauer). Pansy Espy has recorded it in the Davis Mountains on four occasions from August 5 to 31.

BLACKBURNIAN WARBLER. *Dendroica fusca*

There is only one record of this eastern species for the park; the Peckhams and I watched an adult male foraging for insects among the foliage at the beaver pond on the Rio Grande Village Nature Trail, May 6, 1970.

GRACE'S WARBLER. *Dendroica graciae*

Rare migrant. There are three spring records: the earliest

sighting was by Jerry Strickling, a single bird at Rio Grande
Village on May 12, 1962; Philip Allen saw one near the top
of Emory Peak on June 1, 1963; and I found one in Boot
Canyon on May 4, 1967. There are four fall records: I found
one at Boot Canyon on August 8, 1969 (specimen taken),
and August 27, 1967, one at Boot Canyon with several Audubon's and Townsend's warblers on September 24, 1966, and
one in the Basin on August 26, 1969. James Middleton reported one at Boot Springs on September 16, 1970.

CHESTNUT-SIDED WARBLER. *Dendroica pensylvanica*

This little eastern warbler has been recorded in the park
on three occasions. Specimens were taken at Rio Grande Village on May 13 (one of two birds seen) and on October 5,
1969, and I observed another one there on October 10, 1970.

BLACKPOLL WARBLER. *Dendroica striata*

There are three records of this bird for the park. Carl
Swenson first reported one along the river at Rio Grande Village on May 5, 1960; the Harwoods found one flycatching
over the Rio Grande Village silt pond on April 26, 1970; and
I observed one among the oaks at Boot Springs on May 8,
1970.

PALM WARBLER. *Dendroica palmarum*

There is but one record: on April 1, 1970, Joe Lunn, Martin Bovey, and I found a lone bird of the yellow race at Boquillas Crossing. It was collected and represents the first for
the Trans-Pecos.

OVENBIRD. *Seiurus aurocapillus*

Rare spring migrant, and one fall sighting. I found two
birds along the Rio Grande Village Nature Trail on September 11, 1970. Spring records range from April 30 to May 11.
Mr. and Mrs. Kennilee Bates found it first at Boot Springs on
April 30, 1964, and I observed a lone bird at Rio Grande Village on May 1, 1969. In 1970 it was seen on a number of

occasions: Charles Crabtree and I saw one at Boot Springs on May 8, the Peckhams reported one from the Old Ranch on May 9, and I found another along the Rio Grande Village Nature Trail on May 11.

NORTHERN WATERTHRUSH. *Seiurus noveboracensis*

Uncommon migrant in spring and rare in fall. Spring records range from April 20 to May 20 from the river floodplain to the upper Chisos canyons. It usually is seen alone, but three birds were found at Boot Springs on May 4, 1967 (Wauer). It may be more common in spring than records indicate; from May 3 to 17, 1970, I captured and banded four individuals during twelve net-hours at Rio Grande Village. During that same period, I saw only one other Northern Waterthrush. Fall records range from August 22 to September 11: Julius W. Dieckert found one at the Old Ranch on August 29, 1967; Jack Burgess reported one at Boot Springs on September 3, 1956; and I found lone birds at Rio Grande Village on August 22 and 29 and September 11, 1970.

LOUISIANA WATERTHRUSH. *Seiurus motacilla*

There is but one park record. I observed a lone bird near Boquillas Crossing on March 27, 1970. Jody and Clay Miller reported one seen at their ranch in Jeff Davis County in April, 1963.

MacGILLIVRAY'S WARBLER. *Oporornis tolmiei*

Common migrant in spring but rare in fall. Spring records range from April 8 through May 27; it may be numerous along the river floodplain from late April to mid-May. Although most sightings are from the lowlands, it has been recorded in the mountains on a number of occasions. Fall records are sparse from August 31 to September 14.

MOURNING WARBLER. *Oporonis philadelphia*

The only park record of this bird is a sighting along the

Rio Grande Village Nature Trail on April 18, 1972 (Wauer).

YELLOWTHROAT. *Geothlypis trichas*

Fairly common summer resident at localized areas along the river, and common migrant and winter resident. Nesting birds find suitable habitats in reeds and tules along the river and adjacent ponds. A few pairs nest regularly at the silt pond and the beaver pond at Rio Grande Village; two youngsters were seen at the silt pond on July 9, 1968 (Wauer). In migration it is most numerous along the river, but it also has been reported from water areas throughout the park; for example, Allen found one at Boot Canyon on July 31, 1963, and I observed one at Oak Springs on September 9, 1967. Wintering birds can usually be found at areas of heavy vegetation all along the floodplain.

YELLOW-BREASTED CHAT. *Icteria virens*

Abundant summer resident along the river floodplain and less numerous at riparian areas, such as Dugout Wells and the Old Ranch, up to 4,000 feet elevation, and uncommon in migration. It has been recorded from April 10 through September 24, and there is a late sighting of one bird at Boquillas Crossing on November 3, 1967 (Wauer). Early spring arrivals are quiet, but by the end of April this is the most vociferous bird of the floodplain. Displaying birds can be found every few dozen feet wherever there is a heavy growth of vegetation from Lajitas to Stillwell Crossing. By the end of July there is some dispersal of early nesters, but others are still feeding young. By mid-August a very defined decrease in Chats is evident, and they are almost entirely gone from their breeding territories by the end of August. Most September sightings are of late nesters and migrants. There apparently is some movement through the mountains; Walter Boles, Jim Shields, and John St. Julien found a lone bird at Boot Springs on August 10, 1970. There are no other records above 4,000 feet.

HOODED WARBLER. *Wilsonia citrina*

There are four records of this bird for the park. Bill Bromberg and Dr. Baumgartner found it first at Boquillas on November 21, 1961. I have recorded it three times: in upper Pine Canyon on April 30, 1969, and on the Rio Grande Village Nature Trail on May 1 and 3, 1970.

WILSON'S WARBLER. *Wilsonia pusilla*

Abundant migrant from the river floodplain to the top of the Chisos Mountains. This is the park's most common migrant. A few birds reach the area by March 28, and by the second week in April it becomes abundant. A peak is reached from April 22 to 27: more than eighty-five individuals were counted in mesquites within one 125-foot area at Rio Grande Village on April 22, 1970, and more than forty were found at Hot Springs on April 27, 1967 (Wauer). The majority of spring migrants pass through the area by May 20, but stragglers may be found to June 4. Fall migrants have been recorded from August 8 through October 12, and a peak is reached from August 30 to September 19.

CANADA WARBLER. *Wilsonia canadensis*

There are only two park records: Dave Wolf observed a lone female at Boot Spring, feeding in low, damp brush near the corral, on August 23, 1966, and Charles and Ella Newell saw one at Rio Grande Village on May 7, 1971. Pansy Espy has found this bird in the Davis Mountains on three occasions: at Frasier Canyon on August 29, 1968, at the same location with Lou C. Evans on August 29, 1969, and on Pine Peak with H. H. Shugart on April 22, 1970.

AMERICAN REDSTART. *Setophaga ruticilla*

Fairly common migrant from March 28 through June 23 in spring, and from August 25 through September 26 in fall. I also found a lone juvenal female at Rio Grande Village on

October 17, 1970, and the Wilsons and I found one at Cotton-wood Campground on October 24, 1970. Northbound birds reach their peak from May 1 to 23; early and late birds are either females or immature males, but the majority of the early May sightings are adult males. Except for sightings at Boot Springs on May 3, 1961 (Stein), and one from the Old Ranch on May 1, 1967 (Wauer), all spring records are from the lowlands. Fall migrants reach the Big Bend as early as August 25, and a peak is evident from September 5 to 19. The majority of fall birds are either females or immatures.

PAINTED REDSTART. *Setophaga picta*

Uncommon migrant, but it may also be a sporadic summer resident in the higher canyons of the Chisos Mountains. Van Tyne and Sutton (1937) reported that there appear to be "great fluctuations in the numbers " of this bird, and that "in 1901 Bailey, Fuertes, and Oberholser saw no Painted Red-starts during their three weeks' exploration of these mountains (the Chisos during June). In 1928, Van Tyne and Gaige found the species fairly numerous at Boot Spring, and yet Van Tyne, Peet, and Jacot spent the whole of May at the same locality four years later without getting more than an unsatisfactory glimpse of one; and the Carnegie Museum party, in 1933 and 1935, did not record the species at all. On June 24, 1936, however, Tarleton Smith saw an adult male at the head of Blue Creek Canyon."

More recently, Brodrick reported seeing several at Boot Springs on April 3, 1958; Ralph Raitt found it in Pine Canyon on April 16, 1961; David and Roy Brown found one in Boot Canyon on April 28, 1966; David Simon found one there on August 27, 1966; I found two singing birds on Oak Creek, just below the Basin Campground, on March 19, 1967; and Rena Ross, Thelma Fox, Mary Griffith, Margarite Hollar, and Peggy Acord found one at Boot Springs on May 12, 1969. In 1971, the Hurlberts and the Wauers found one at Rio Grande Village on March 20 (the only lowland record for the park), and I found singing birds in Boot Canyon on April 10, 18, and 24.

This is a common nesting bird of the forested slopes of the del Carmen Mountains of Coahuila, Mexico, fifty miles southeast of the Chisos. It is possible that some years it also nests in the Chisos highlands.

WEAVER FINCHES: Family Ploceidae

HOUSE SPARROW. *Passer domesticus*

Common resident at areas of human habitation: Rio Grande Village, Castolon, Panther Junction, and the Chisos Basin. Van Tyne and Sutton reported one taken at Glenn Springs on July 26, 1928, which represented the first for the park area. It is of some interest that this species no longer resides at Glenn Springs, probably because of the present lack of human occupation there. This may be one of the few instances on record that the House Sparrow deserted an area; records are usually of invasions. Tarleton Smith reported in 1936 that, although the species was present at Boquillas and settlements along the Rio Grande, "none have found our camp in the Basin." The area of the Basin Campground, Remuda, and Lodge is now one of the House Sparrow strongholds. In 1963, Allen reported that he found only "4 pairs" of House Sparrows at Panther Junction. A conservative estimate of the 1970 population there exceeded two hundred birds; during one week in May, 1970, thirty-four birds were collected for use as practice skins for a class in ornithology at Sul Ross State University in Alpine. The reduction of House Sparrows was not evident. It is impossible to estimate how long the species has been in the Big Bend area, but Montgomery (1905) reported it as common at Alpine as early as June, 1904.

House Sparrows in the park apparently are quite mobile. Birds banded at Panther Junction also frequent the Basin Remuda. Rio Grande Village House Sparrows spend most of their time there in winter and spring, but are most numerous at Boquillas, Mexico, during summer and fall.

MEADOWLARKS, BLACKBIRDS, and ORIOLES: Family Icteridae

EASTERN MEADOWLARK. *Sturnella magna*

Uncommon migrant and winter visitor. The Eastern and Western meadowlarks are so similar that it is impossible to tell them apart without a specimen or hearing them sing. The Eastern Meadowlark's call is five or six clear whistles; that of the Western Meadowlark is loud and flutelike, the call heard in western movies. As a child growing up in Idaho, I was told that the meadowlark said, *Salt Lake City is a pretty lit-tle city.* The Eastern Meadowlark nests throughout the open grasslands from Marathon to Fort Stockton and Alpine to Balmorhea. It has not been found to nest within the lower part of Brewster County, but it does frequent this area during the fall, winter, and spring. It apparently overwinters within the Sotol-grasslands and on grassy flats along the river. Road-kills examined on September 26, 1967, October 6, 1968, December 21, 1967, and January 27, 1968, from Panther Junction to the lower Tornillo Creek bridge, proved to be this species. It was taken on the South Rim on May 20, 1932 (Van Tyne and Sutton), and a flock of twelve to fourteen birds at the Rio Grande Village Campground in March, 1967, were identified by their songs (Russ and Marion Wilson).

WESTERN MEADOWLARK. *Sturnella neglecta*

Fairly common migrant and winter resident. Like the eastern form, this bird can be found within the lower Sotol-grasslands and the grassy flats adjacent to the Rio Grande during fall, winter, and spring. It has been recorded from October 9 through May 4 but apparently does not nest within the lower Big Bend area, although Dale Zimmerman found what he believes to have been a nesting bird near the K-Bar Ranch the second week of April. 1971. It does nest in the higher valleys of the Davis Mountains. Road-kills found from Panther Junction to Rio Grande Village on October 15, 1967, December 2, 1967, February 1, 1969, and March 14, 1967, proved to be this species. It sometimes can be found in quite large flocks; I found sixty-five or more birds near San Vicente on November 11, 1967. Brodrick reported it at Panther Junction on January 17, March 9, and April 5, 1961. Several singing birds at Rio Grande Village on March 8, 1970, were of this species (Wauer).

YELLOW-HEADED BLACKBIRD. *Xanthocephalus xanthocephalus*

Fairly common migrant and rare in winter. This large blackbird has been reported for the park every month but February and March. Spring migrants pass through the area from April 12 to May 31; they may be found alone with a flock of Brewer's Blackbirds or Brown-headed Cowbirds, or in small to large unmixed flocks. One hundred and twenty males were seen at Rio Grande Village on April 25, 1969 (Wauer), the Whitsons reported a mixed flock of twenty-five to thirty birds there on April 30, 1968, and the Hotchkisses saw a lone male at the top of the Lost Mine Trail (6,900 feet) on May 20, 1970. Except for one sighting of a lone bird at Grapevine Spring by Dixon, June 14, 1956, there are no records for the park from May 31 through July 6.

Southbound birds may appear in mixed or pure flocks of males early in summer; there are several sightings of 3 to 10 males at Panther Junction on July 8 and 9, and Brodrick found a flock of more than 100 birds there on July 23, 1957. I found a mixed flock of about 30 birds at Solis on July 23, 1970. There are several reports of a few to many Yellow-heads from mid-August to October 3; I observed a flock of more than 235 birds at Panther Junction on September 12, 1969, and Youse found it at Maverick on September 12 and 24, 1961. Although there are only two wintertime records for the park—Robert Tanhope observed one along the river near Black Dike on December 4, 1969, and Bruce McHenry reported one at Panther Junction on January 10, 1955—it can usually be found with flocks of blackbirds at fields and corrals throughout the northern part of the Big Bend Country all winter.

REDWINGED BLACKBIRD. *Agelaius phoeniceus*

Uncommon migrant from February 25 to May 15 in spring and from August 16 to November 19 in fall. It is surprisingly rare, even along the river, where there appear to be suitable nesting sites. The largest flock yet reported for the park is the thirty birds seen by Van Tyne and Sutton at Castolon on February 25, 1935. In recent years, the largest reported flocks were of eight birds at Rio Grande Village on April 28, 1967 (Wauer), and more than ten near Santa Elena Canyon on August 19, 1971 (Easterla). Most sightings are of one or two individuals with a flock of Brewer's or Yellow-headed blackbirds; I found two with more than twenty Yellow-heads at Rio Grande Village on September 6, 1968. There are only two records away from the vicinity of the river; David Simon found four at the Basin Campground on August 27, 1966, and Sharon Wauer saw one at Panther Junction on November 19, 1967.

ORCHARD ORIOLE. *Icterus spurius*

Abundant summer resident at Rio Grande Village but less common along the rest of the floodplain. It has been recorded as early as April 11 and as late as September 28. This is a very gregarious species, and the birds spend the early part of the breeding season chasing one another around their territories. Only males are known to sing; second-year males sing and nest as well. Nesting occurs during May, June, and July, although I found an adult Orchard Oriole feeding a young Bronzed Cowbird on July 28, 1970. There is considerable post-nesting wandering, particularly among immature birds, and they may be found to 4,500 feet elevation. One was seen along the lower part of the Window Trail on July 9, 1962, and they are regular at Panther Junction and adjacent washes from late July to early September. Females and immature birds were banded at Panther Junction on July 21, 1970, August 6 and 20, 1967, September 7, 1967, and September 20, 1969. By early September this bird becomes rare on its breeding grounds; I have seen only one adult male later than the first of September, although adult females and immatures can usually be found with some effort.

HOODED ORIOLE. *Icterus cucullatus*

Fairly common summer resident at Rio Grande Village and the adjacent floodplain but less common elsewhere along the river, and rare migrant. It has been recorded from March 16 through October 1. Adult males arrive on their breeding grounds the last of March and the first of April, and it is several days before females and sub-adults put in their appearance. Like the Orchard Oriole, Hooded Orioles are very gregarious at first and can often be found chasing other Hooded Orioles and Orchard Orioles. Nest-building begins by mid-May; the earliest nest-building I have found was at Rio Grande Village on May 11, 1970. Young are fledged in June and July; adults were found feeding nestlings on May 24, 1969, two fledged birds were seen at Rio Grande Village on July 17, 1968, and a nest containing two young Bronzed Cowbirds was discovered there in a Tamarisk on July 12, 1970 (Wauer). Apparently, there is also some late nesting; I found a new nest under construction near the top of a tall cottonwood at Rio Grande Village on July 18, 1970.

Post-nesting birds do not seem to wander as much as Orchard Orioles, although there appears to be some movement into the mountains; I found an adult male feeding at a Century Plant near the Basin Campground on August 1, 1966, and one female at Juniper Flat on August 10, 1969. Migrants have been recorded on only a few occasions. It is assumed that early birds in mid-March are migrants; I found adult males at Panther Junction on March 19, 1967, and April 17,

1970. Fall migrants are few in the mountains; I found only one in the Basin on October 1, 1966.

SCOTT'S ORIOLE. *Icterus parisorum*

Common summer resident of the yucca-Sotol-grasslands, common migrant, and may remain until the first severe cold front reaches the Big Bend. There is a lapse of records only from January 17 to March 6. Adult males arrive first; singing males were recorded in lower Green Gulch on March 19, 1969, and at the Basin on April 17, 1968 (Wauer). Females and sub-adults arrive a few days later, and nesting begins immediately rather than being preceded by a period of play, as is the case with the Orchard and Hooded orioles. Nesting has been recorded at Panther Junction as early as March 23, 1960 (Brodrick); Van Tyne and Sutton reported young already out of the nest at Boquillas on May 16, 1933; I found a nest on a Torrey Yucca near Santa Elena Canyon on April 28, 1968, and banded three nestlings at the Basin on June 8, 1970. This last nest was located on a Beaked Yucca in front of the motel unit. Another nest was built within a few inches of the first one and young were seen on August 9; I assumed that it belonged to the same adults.

The post-nesting period appears to be the main time for play for this oriole, and there is some flocking; a flock of fifteen birds (five adults and ten immatures) was seen along the Window Trail on September 10, 1967 (Wauer). Family groups of three to seven birds are more common and are sometimes found considerably above their nesting grounds. I recorded lone birds at Laguna Meadow (6,300 feet) on September 4, 1967, and September 8, 1969, and an adult male and two females at 7,000 feet at the end of the Lost Mine Trail on October 26, 1968. Some birds remain on their breeding grounds throughout the fall and early winter. Seven individuals were seen along Oak Creek just below the Basin Campground on December 1, 1968, and three were found there on December 23. Apparently, it may even stay throughout the winter; I found an immature male on the open mesquite flat near Boquillas Canyon on December 29, 1970, and January 16, 1971.

BALTIMORE ORIOLE. *Icterus galbula*

There is but one record of this eastern oriole; Dixon and Wallmo (1956) collected one at Black Gap on June 20, 1955.

BULLOCK'S ORIOLE. *Icterus bullockii*

Uncommon migrant from April 3 to May 15 in spring and from July 29 through October 3 in fall. There is also a summer sighting at Boquillas on June 21, 1936 (Tarleton Smith), and James Scudday collected an adult male along Alamo Creek, seventeen miles southeast of Marfa, on June 10, 1968. The majority of park sightings are of lone birds, but five (two adult males and three females or immatures) individuals were found on the Rio Grande Village Nature Trail on August 20 and 22, 1970 (Wauer). Although the majority of records are from the lowlands, there is one from Boot Springs on April 12, 1956 (Brodrick), one from Laguna Meadow on May 6, 1968 (Ned Fritz), one from the Chisos Basin on August 31, 1967, and one from Lost Mine Trail on September 19, 1967 (Wauer). There is no evidence of nesting within the park, and Pansy Espy has not found the bird summering in the Davis Mountains. It is a common summer resident in the El Paso area and eastward along the river (McBee and Keefer, 1967).

BLACK-VENTED ORIOLE. *Icterus wagleri*

A single adult female was seen at Rio Grande Village between mid-April and early October in 1969 and 1970 (Wauer, 1970*b*). It was first discovered on September 27, 1968; I watched it for several minutes among the foliage of the thicket of vegetation along the nature trail. The black crissum and other characteristics were later compared to oriole identities in Blake (1953) and Sutton (1951), and I was able to identify it without doubt as Wagler's Oriole, or Black-vented Oriole, as is preferred by the American Ornithologists' Union. I could not find it on the following morning.

On April 28, 1969, an adult Wagler's again was seen less than three hundred feet from the first sighting. For more than forty minutes I watched it and six other orioles (an adult female and an immature male Hooded Oriole, and two females and an adult and immature male Orchard Oriole) chase each other from tree to tree within the Rio Grande Village Campground. The Wagler's Oriole appeared to be in close association with the immature male Hooded Oriole, which nicely fit Sutton's description of a female Wagler. Although I have since learned that the species is monomorphic, having a single color pattern, I assumed that this was a possible nesting pair. On May 1, I again observed the Wagler's Oriole at the same location with, assumedly, the same six orioles.

Also on May 1, I met Ty and Julie Hotchkiss, who were camped at Rio Grande Village. When I informed them of the bird's identity, they graciously offered to photograph the bird for further documentation. During the following three weeks they took more than fifty feet of 16 mm movie film and eight color slides. *I. wagleri* was further authenticated by the observation of several persons as follows: Mr. and Mrs. H. T. Hargis (they also obtained excellent photographs), Terry Hall, Kay McCracken, Doris Maguire, Russ and Marion Wilson, Doyle and Helen Peckham, Warren and Bobby Pulich, Charles and Betty Crabtree, Dave Wolf, James Tucker, Doug Eddleman, and Mike Parmeter in May; David Easterla, Guy McCaskie, Cliff Lyons, and Ginger Coughran in June; and Bob Smith and Paul Sykes in July.

These data represent the first authentic records of the Wagler's Oriole for the United States, although there is a questionable sighting by Herbert Brown from the Patagonia Mountains, Arizona, in 1910 (Phillips, 1968). South of the border it occurs "from Sonora, Chihuahua, and Nuevo Leon, south through Guatemala and Honduras to El Salvador (in winter) and northern Nicaragua" (Freidman, Griscom, and Moore, 1957). The Mexican records nearest to Big Bend National Park are those from the state of Coahuila, where Charles Ely (1962) studied the avifauna in the southeastern part of the state. Birds seen 15 miles southwest of Gómez Farias represent the breeding records of *I. wagleri* nearest the Big Bend, a distance of about 350 airline miles.

By mid-May it was evident that the Wagler's Oriole at Rio Grande Village was not nesting, and that there was no more than a single bird. Its behavior gave no indication that it was defending a territory. Yet, by mid-morning it would usually disappear into the dense floodplain vegetation and often did not return to the campground portion of its range until late afternoon or evening. By 6:30 A.M. it was always back in the campground with many immature Orchards or one or two immature Hooded Orioles that were still present. All these seemed to prefer the fruits of the Squaw-Bush, which were ripening throughout May and June. On May 19 I watched *I. wagleri* feed on flowers of Desertwillow for several minutes. And on June 28 it caught a cicada, tore the wings off, and consumed the softer parts of the body, dropping the harder parts to the ground.

In order to obtain close-up photographs for racial identification, as well as to band the bird so that it would be recognized if it returned again, I made several attempts to net it between June 28 and July 4. On July 1, I placed a mounted Great Horned Owl, a species that occurs commonly in the immediate vicinity, on the ground next to a mist net. *I. wagleri* perched ten feet above the stuffed bird and watched while a pair of Mockingbirds launched attack after attack on the owl until both Mockers were caught in the netting. I even drew a Wagler's Oriole on paper, colored it with the proper colors, and mounted the drawing on a stick next to the net. This, too, was a failure. The only reaction obtained from *I. wagleri* was one of vague curiosity. Yet it did show interest in people on a number of occasions. Several times I observed it watching campers going about their routine camp duties, and on one occasion it flew into a tree above two children who were rolling a red rubber ball around on the ground. It sat there watching this action for about four minutes before flying off to another perch. On only two occasions did I observe it showing any aggression toward another bird, and then only two very short chases (fifteen to twenty feet) of female Orchard Orioles. Although *I. wagleri* could usually be detected by a very low, rasping call, like that of a Yellow-breasted Chat or Scott's Oriole, a song was never heard.

Finally, by moving the nets each time *I. wagleri* changed positions, I succeeded in capturing it on July 4. Closer examination showed that it was in nonbreeding status; it clearly lacked evidence of a brood patch and had no cloacal protuberance. Close examination of the bill and cere showed no indication that the bird had been caged at any time. Close-up photographs of the chest were sent to Allan Phillips, who identified the bird racially as the *wagleri* form of eastern Mexico. The chest had a light chestnut tinge.

After carefully photographing the major features of the bird, I placed a band (No. 632–25253) on its right leg and released it. It immediately flew south to the floodplain portion of the range, dived into the dense vegetation, and was not seen the rest of the day. By July 10, however, it was right back in its same habits and allowed good binocular examination the first half of each morning.

By early August it became quite shy and had to be searched for among the dense foliage along the nature trail. I last saw it on September 19, 1969, exactly one year after the original date of discovery. In 1970, I found it again in the same locality from April 17 through September 21 and again on October 10. A goodly number of birders found the same banded bird from the previous year throughout the summer.

RUSTY BLACKBIRD. *Euphagus carolinus*

Rare fall visitor. The first park sighting was collected along an irrigation ditch at Rio Grande Village on December 10, 1967 (Wauer, 1969*b*). John Galley observed one at Hot Springs on December 27, 1967, two were seen with a flock of ten Brewer's Blackbirds and eight Brown-headed Cowbirds at Rio Grande Village on October 27, 1968, and another was seen near the beaver pond on December 23, 1970 (Wauer).

BREWER'S BLACKBIRD. *Euphagus cyanocephalus*

Common migrant and rare winter visitor. Spring migrants have been recorded from March 21 through May 27; early arrivals are usually alone or in twos or threes, but by April 12 flocks of 10 to 25 birds are more common. The peak of the spring migration is April 26 to May 6, and flocks of 6 to 120 (recorded at Rio Grande Village on April 28, 1967) can be found moving along the river throughout the daytime hours. Most migrants are pretty well confined to the river and lowlands, but sightings in the mountains are not uncommon. I have seen birds at a number of places in the Chisos Mountains: a lone male at the end of the Lost Mine Trail on March 21, 1967, several at the sewage lagoons on April 26, 1968, and April 26, 1969, and four flocks of 15 to 28 birds over the Basin on May 4, 1968. The Brewer's is a fairly common visitor to Panther Junction from April 12 to May 27; 7 birds were banded there from April 17 to May 1, 1970, but only 2 in the fall—on September 21, 1970, and October 3, 1969. Fall migrants reach the park area during the first week of September, and the southward trend continues at a regular pace until late October. A few stragglers continue to pass through the area until late December. There is one January record of a lone male seen along the Black Gap road just north of the park on January 21, 1970 (Wauer). This species occurs at fields and corrals throughout the northern part of the Big Bend in winter, and Pansy Espy has found it nesting in the Davis Mountains.

GREAT-TAILED GRACKLE. *Cassidix mexicanus*

Uncommon along the river in spring, and rare in summer, fall, and winter. Its nesting status is questionable. H. Lee Watson found a pair in the floodplain vegetation near Black

Dike, on June 10, 1970, and suspected nesting; it is present at Lajitas throughout the year. This bird may be on the increase. It was reported first at Castolon by Van Tyne and Sutton on May 6 and 7, 1933. Adele Harding next recorded it at Rio Grande Village on June 10, 1965. From April 1 through June 12 in spring, I have found it regularly in the vicinity of Rio Grande Village and Cottonwood Campground. Wintering birds probably are visitors from across the river, where they occur throughout the winter at Santa Elena, Chihuahua; I found a flock of twenty-two at Cottonwood Campground on December 21. 1967, and six on December 30, 1968. This is the Boat-tailed Grackle of earlier publication; the taxonomy was revised by Selander and Giller (1961).

BROWN-HEADED COWBIRD. *Molothrus ater*

Abundant summer resident along the floodplain. at Panther Junction, and in the Chisos Basin. and less numerous elsewhere below 5,500 feet. and common migrant and rare winter visitor. Breeding birds belong to the small *obscurus* race of cowbirds that is sometimes referred to as the "Dwarf Cowbird." They arrive on their breeding grounds during the first and second weeks of April, and parasitize a great number of the park's smaller nesting species. including the Black-tailed Gnatcatcher, Bell's Vireo, Yellow-breasted Chat. House Sparrow, Blue Grosbeak, Painted Bunting, and Black-throated Sparrow. All breeding birds above 2,500 feet elevation in the Chisos Mountains may be one huge flock; birds banded at Panther Junction have been regularly recorded in the Basin. Adult "Dwarf Cowbirds" move out of their breeding grounds the last week of July but are replaced immediately by a larger race (*artemisae*) during the first week of August. Some of the local youngsters intermingle with the larger birds, which may remain until early September. By mid-September only an occasional migrant is to be found.

Spring migrants have been recorded along the river and in the lowlands from March 17 to early June. Early arrivals usually are alone or in small flocks, but many larger flocks can be found when the main movement gets underway, from the first of April to mid-May. Northbound birds are most numerous in the lowlands but occasionally are seen at Laguna Meadow, Boot Canyon, and the South Rim in late May and early June. Fall migrants have not been recorded above 5,500 feet elevation. Flocks of a few to thirty birds occur regularly to mid-September, and a few stragglers have been recorded until October 27. There are no November records, but a rare winter visitor was seen at Panther Junction in late December and January. Brown-headed Cowbirds winter with Brewer's Blackbirds throughout the northern Big Bend Country.

BRONZED COWBIRD. *Tangavius aeneus*

Local summer visitor only since 1969. On June 9, 1969, Easterla found four males and two females at Rio Grande Village; one of the males was courting two females. The species was last seen on July 4 in 1969 (Wauer). It was recorded on June 8 in 1970 (Easterla), and at least six males and four females stayed in the Rio Grande Village Campground area until July 3. On July 12 I found a Hooded Oriole nest, hanging on a Tamarisk near the Daniel house, that contained two juvenal Bronzed Cowbirds (one was collected). On July 18 the nest was empty and a juvenal Bronzed Cowbird was found fifty-five feet away being fed by both adult Hooded Orioles. On July 28 I discovered another young Bronzed Cowbird at an Orchard Oriole nest near the large pond; Easterla and I watched the youngster being fed by the adult female Orchard Oriole on July 30.

In 1971, an adult male appeared at Panther Junction on May 22, and remained until May 29, when it was banded and released; it did not return. I found four males and four females at Rio Grande Village on May 29, and at least a few of these individuals remained through July 13; a juvenal Bronzed Cowbird was seen begging from an Orchard Oriole on August 4. Also in 1971, I found it present at Cottonwood Campground from June 5 through July 10.

It appears that this species is increasing within the Big Bend area and will probably become a regular breeding bird, as it is in the lower Rio Grande Valley. If this is the case, it is likely that the population of breeding Orchard and Hooded orioles along the floodplain will decrease.

TANAGERS: Family Thraupidae
WESTERN TANAGER. *Piranga ludoviciana*

Rare in summer and a fairly common migrant. Tarleton Smith reported seeing "young birds barely able to fly" in Pine Canyon on July 24, 1936. There is no recent evidence that this is a breeding bird of the Chisos Mountains, in spite of a vigorously singing adult male seen at Juniper Flat on June 7, 1970 (Wauer). Northbound birds may reach the Big Bend area as early as late February; Ann LeSassier and Phil Allen found two males on the Window Trail, February 27, 1963. There are no March records, but this bird becomes regular after April 18. Spring migrants reach a peak from May 6 to 15, and stragglers have been recorded as late as May 26. Except for the one June sighting above, there are no other park records until July 4, when post-nesting or non-breeding birds become regular in occurrence. I found adult males at Rio Grande Village on July 4, 1969, and July 12, 1970. It is more common within the mountains, where birds can be found throughout the rest of the summer. Southbound birds have been recorded regularly during September and decrease in early October; stragglers have been recorded until October 25.

SCARLET TANAGER. *Piranga olivacea*

Rare spring visitor from April 26 to May 29. It was first reported for the park by Ola Haynes, Doris Williams, and June and Francis Kingon, who found one at Dugout Wells on May 20, 1962. Mrs. Carl Swenson saw one at Rio Grande Village on May 6, 1966; I saw a lone male there on April 26,

1967; and John and Ethelyne Bizilo and Mrs. L. Q. Reese reported one from the Santa Elena Canyon picnic area on May 29, 1967.

HEPATIC TANAGER. *Piranga flava*

Uncommon summer resident above 5,000 feet in the Chisos Mountains from May 1 through September 25. Although this species is never numerous, it occurs regularly at a few localities. Pairs can usually be found just above the Basin cottages and along the start of the South Rim Trail, in the vicinity of Juniper Flat and the water storage tank, along the second mile of the South Rim Trail, between the South Rim Trail just above Laguna Meadow and Boot Springs, and near the upper water barrel in Green Gulch. Singing birds can usually be heard from the Basin cottages almost any morning in May. I found a nest on a Pinyon Pine near the Lodge on May 12, 1968, and an adult male was seen carrying food near there on June 10, 1967. Lowland records are questionable; I have never found this tanager below the Chisos woodlands. Fall birds can be very confusing because the bill color of the Summer Tanager can be very dark in fall. The liverred color of the Hepatic Tanager male is the only positive field characteristic in fall.

SUMMER TANAGER. *Piranga rubra*

Abundant at Rio Grande Village and Cottonwood Camp ground and less numerous elsewhere on the floodplain and at riparian areas up to 5,000 feet. Males arrive as early as April 1, and females and sub-adults follow within a week or two. By the last week of April it is abundant at Rio Grande Village; I counted forty there on April 23, 1967. It does not reach its breeding territories in the mountain canyons until late April. It nests along the river and at such places as Dugout Wells, the Old Ranch, and within the deciduous vegetation along the lower canyons—for example, at Cattail Falls, Oak Creek, and Green Gulch. During the summers of 1968 and 1969 the feeding territories of this species and the Hepatic Tanager overlapped along the drainage of Oak Creek just below the Basin Campground.

Summer Tanagers are very gregarious and, like the Orchard and Hooded orioles that use the same cottonwood groves at Rio Grande Village, they spend a great deal of time chasing each other around the grove when they first arrive. Nesting gets underway by early May, and young are out of the nest in June, although there is some late nesting as well; nest-building was found at Rio Grande Village on June 20, 1967, and adults were seen feeding young in the nest at Boquillas Crossing on August 20, 1970 (Wauer). I have detected only minor post-nesting wandering; for the most part, this species seems to remain on the breeding grounds throughout August and most of September. There is a noticeable decrease in birds by the last of September, and I could find only two individuals at Rio Grande Village on October 5, 1969. The latest sighting is of a lone bird along Oak Creek on October 10, 1967 (Wauer).

GROSBEAKS, BUNTINGS, FINCHES, and SPARROWS: Family Fringillidae

CARDINAL. *Richmondena cardinalis*

Common in summer and winter at localized areas along the floodplain (e.g., along the Rio Grande Village Nature Trail), and less numerous elsewhere along the river and at adjacent riparian areas up to 3,500 feet elevation, and an uncommon migrant. Breeding birds can also be found some summers at Dugout Wells, Government Spring, and the Old Ranch. Most sightings away from the river and other water areas are probably migrants. Small flocks of ten to fifteen birds were seen moving north near Rio Grande Village on March 21, 1969; a lone male was found at Panther Junction on March 19, 1967; and two females were seen at Government Spring on March 20, 1971 (Wauer). Hank Schmidt saw a Cardinal at Panther Junction on September 16, 1960;

one stayed there from November 29, 1967, to December 13, 1968, and was banded on December 9 (Wauer).

PYRRHULOXIA. *Pyrrhuloxia sinuata*

Common summer and winter resident, and uncommon migrant. This is a bird of the desert washes; the look-alike Cardinal prefers riparian areas. Pyrrhuloxias can usually be found at mesquite-acacia thickets along the drier parts of the floodplain and in arroyos and canyons up to 4,500 feet elevation. Lowland birds are mostly permanent residents. Nesting occurs in April, May, and June; I found adults feeding young at Rio Grande Village on May 21, 1968, and a nest seven feet high on a mesquite there on June 14, 1968. Pyrrhuloxias are fairly shy while nesting but become easy to find again right afterward. Except for the resident birds of the floodplain, there appears to be considerable wandering after nesting. It becomes quite numerous at Panther Junction and in the Chisos Basin during late July and August. By October, birds may be found in the higher parts of the mountains as well; I saw two in upper Boot Canyon on October 22, 1967, and one near the South Rim on November 4, 1967. Wintering records are all below 5,000 feet. Most resident birds congregate into flocks of ten to thirty birds from late September through the first of March. Those in the lower mountain canyons seldom flock, but are usually found in groups of three or four.

ROSE-BREASTED GROSBEAK. *Pheucticus ludovicianus*

Rare spring migrant from April 7 to May 13. Most records are from the mountains, at Boot Canyon, Laguna Meadow, and Oak Creek, but there also are three lowland sightings: lone males were seen at Rio Grande Village on May 3, 1970, and May 12, 1969 (Wauer), and at the Old Ranch on May 10, 1970 (the Peckhams).

BLACK-HEADED GROSBEAK. *Pheucticus melanocephalus*

Common summer resident in the mountains and uncommon migrant. This is a bird of the deciduous woodlands above 4,500 feet elevation. It reaches the Big Bend the last week of April (April 25) and begins to nest almost immediately; I found it nest-building in the Chisos Basin on May 2, 1967, and Tarleton Smith reported a nest with two well-feathered young in the Basin on July 11, 1936. Breeding birds begin to move out of the area by early September, and by the middle of the month only migrants can be found. I found a late southbound bird along the Window Trail on October 4, 1968, and an immature bird visited my feeder at Panther Junction on November 4 and 5, 1969. One seen by Sperry and Galliger in the Basin on December 21, 1960, was a very late vagrant. Most of the park's Black-headed Grosbeak records are from the mountains, but there is a handful of sightings from the lowlands; I found lone males at Rio Grande Village on May 8, 1968, May 6, 1970, September 14, 1969, September 19, 1968, and September 26, 1969.

BLUE GROSBEAK. *Guiraca caerulea*

Fairly common summer resident and uncommon migrant. Like the Black-headed Grosbeak of the mountains, this species is one of the late spring arrivals. Migrants begin to move along the Rio Grande the last week of April (the earliest sighting is April 26), but they do not become regular until the first of May. The Blue Grosbeak nests in riparian thickets along the river, at a few of the dense mesquite bosques in desert arroyos, and along mountain drainages to 5,000 feet. It can almost always be found in summer along the Rio Grande Village Nature Trail, at the Old Ranch, and along Oak Creek below the Basin Campground. Nest-building was recorded at Rio Grande Village on June 10, 1970 (Easterla). By early August, many of the brightly colored males are in molt. This, combined with the worn plumage, presents a very mottled bird looking very much like the juvenals that trail after the adults as they feed in weedy patches adjacent to the thickets. It may appear that the breeding grounds are practically deserted because of their habits of feeding elsewhere. Fall migrants begin to replace resident birds during the last week of August and reach a peak the first few days of September. Stragglers continue to pass through the area until October 1.

INDIGO BUNTING. *Passerina cyanea*

Uncommon spring migrant from April 24 to June 10, and irregular summer visitor until July 4. There appear to be two separate spring movements through the Big Bend. The first series of records range from April 24 to May 13; there are no sightings from May 14 to 17; and another movement is evident from May 18 to 26. Although most of these records are from the lowlands, this bird has been reported regularly near the Basin Campground and along the Window Trail. In 1968, two singing males were seen on June 22 and 27 along the lower end of the Window Trail. They appeared to be competing for territories with Varied Buntings that were very vocal within the immediate vicinity. And in 1970, singing male Indigos were found at Rio Grande Village from May 22 to June 10, in the same area as singing Painted Buntings. In both cases, the Indigo Buntings left the territories to the Varied and Painted buntings. There is also a July 4, 1967, sighting of an adult male Indigo on the Rio Grande Village Nature Trail (Wauer). I found the Indigo Bunting only once after July—an immature male at Rio Grande Village on September 18, 1970.

LAZULI BUNTING. *Passerina amoena*

Rare migrant in spring from May 2 to 11, and only two fall sightings. I found three males near Santa Elena Canyon on September 2, 1968, and one was reported from Pine Canyon on September 20, 1956. All spring sightings are from the lowlands, except one found by Brodrick in the Chisos Basin on May 2 and 3, 1958.

VARIED BUNTING. *Passerina versicolor*

Fairly common summer resident and spring migrant, and

one winter sighting. I found a lone adult male just below the Basin Campground on December 28, 1968. The earliest records include an adult male seen at Rio Grande Village on April 4, 1972 (Wauer and the Wilsons), and one caught in a mist net at Panther Junction on April 18, 1969; it was banded and released. During the first two weeks of May, Varied Buntings become fairly common over the desert, particularly along washes and at weedy places along the roads. Males apparently arrive on their breeding grounds first and are later followed by the females; on April 29, 1970, I found four singing males along the Window Trail, but no females could be found. A male was actively defending a territory in this same area on May 24, 1968, and a male was seen feeding two youngsters there on July 19, 1969. I found a nest with three young in Blue Creek Canyon on June 4, 1968, and seven singing males within one mile of Cottonwood Wash, just behind the Old Ranch, on July 13, 1968. Four singing males, and one nest on a Squaw-Bush, were found along one mile of Blue Creek Canyon, just above the Wilson Ranch house, on June 4, 1968. It also can be found in summer in the little wash just below Government Spring; and on June 5, 1970, I found four singing birds among the rather open mesquite thickets north of the roadway northeast of Todd Hill. Apparently, there is double-brooding or late nesting as well. I found an adult male feeding two fledged young along the Window Trail on August 28, 1966; and on August 23, 1970, I found nine singing males and several females and immature birds along a two-mile stretch of lower Panther Canyon. A visit there on September 13 turned up only two adult males, but one was feeding three very recenty fledged youngsters. It appears that the Varied Bunting is quite numerous during wet years, but less common during years of little precipitation. During the wet summer of 1968, I found a singing male within a thicket of mesquite and reeds along the river, just two miles below Santa Elena Canyon. And on August 11, 1971, Red and Marjorie Adams and Roseann Rose found an adult male feeding young below the Santa Elena Canyon overlook. There appears to be some post-nesting wandering along the washes. but the bird can usually be found with some searching in the proper habitat until mid-September.

PAINTED BUNTING. *Passerina ciris*

Abundant summer resident at Rio Grande Village, common elsewhere along the floodplain and less numerous at springs and water areas up to 3.500 feet elevation in summer, and rare spring migrant. This is another rather late spring arrival; the earliest sighting is April 4 (Easterla), but it is not until April 24 that it suddenly is common along the floodplain. Nesting occurs during June, July, and August, but males move away from their breeding territories during the first two weeks of August. Only females and immature birds are usually seen afterward. By early September, females and young are also often hard to find, but a search through nearby weed patches will usually result in the finding of a few. Immature birds can usually be found at such places until October 5.

Fall migrants are rare; an adult male found on the Rio Grande Nature Trail on September 21, 1970, was an assumed migrant because it was the first adult male seen there since August 22. There is also an extremely late sighting of a lone female at Rio Grande Village on November 19, 1970 (Wauer). Spring migrants are somewhat more numerous; I found lone birds at the Old Ranch on May 4 and 23, 1968, and banded an adult female at Panther Junction on May 21, 1970.

DICKCISSEL. *Spiza americana*

Uncommon migrant. There were no records of this bird prior to 1967, when one appeared at my feeder at Panther Junction on May 14. Since then I have found it regularly from April 26 to May 24 in spring and from August 14 to October 15 in fall. Three were banded at Panther Junction in 1967, on September 7, 8, and 10, none in 1968, two in 1969, on August 29 and September 1; five birds were banded at Rio Grande Village on September 20, 1969; and none in 1970. Most records are of small flocks of two to five birds. I cannot help wondering whether this species is only beginning to move through the Big Bend Country or was just missed in earlier years.

CASSIN'S FINCH. *Carpodacus cassinii*

Irregular visitor to the Chisos highlands any time of year. It has been recorded every month but May and September. Apparently, it is somewhat sporadic in occurrence. It was seen several times in 1966–67: I found one in the Basin on August 13; Leon Bishop reported a "flock of about one dozen" in the pines on Lost Mine Ridge on October 20; and I found two there on November 6, two more at the South Rim on January 29, one at Boot Springs on March 30, one flying over the Basin on April 2 and 6, and one at Boot Springs on June 8. Since then it has been recorded only once: I found a lone male near Laguna Meadow on July 20, 1969.

HOUSE FINCH. *Carpodacus mexicanus*

Common resident below 5,500 feet elevation, and common spring migrant. At least a few can be found almost any place below 5,500 feet at any time of the year. Nesting begins early on the desert and fledged birds can be found by late April or early May. During wet years it may nest in July and August as well. Of special interest was a nest built in an abandoned Cliff Swallow nest at Hot Springs on March 29, 1968. Post-nesting birds occasionally wander into the higher canyons, such as Boot Canyon, where I found it on August 10, 1968. For the most part, it is restricted to lower areas. Family groups become the nucleus of flocks that may number 50 to 150 birds during fall, winter, and spring. There is a considerable increase in House Finches during a brief period from mid-March through mid-April in spring.

PINE SISKIN. *Spinus pinus*

Fairly common migrant and uncommon winter visitor.

The earliest fall record is a flock of seventeen birds seen by David Wolf in the Chisos Basin on August 19, 1968. It is rarely seen during September and the first of October but becomes more numerous after October 20. There are many late-November and December sightings, and it is seen regularly from the Rio Grande floodplain to the top of the Chisos throughout the winter. By late March there is a slight increase of sightings; this early build-up subsides somewhat in mid-April but increases again during the first two weeks of May. In fact, large flocks of Pine Siskins may remain through mid-May, but by late May only a few stragglers remain. Lone birds were seen at Boot Canyon on June 8, 1970, and at Rio Grande Village on June 9, 1970 (Wauer). Charles Bender found it nesting at Madera Park, Davis Mountains, on June 6, 1970.

AMERICAN GOLDFINCH. *Spinus tristis*

Fairly common spring migrant and uncommon in fall and winter. It has been recorded every month but June and July. The earliest fall record is one collected at Oak Creek on September 8, 1956 (Texas A&M), but it does not occur regularly until the last of October, after which a few individuals can usually be found along the river and in the mountain canyons throughout the winter. Flocks of fifteen to thirty birds are most common, but a flock of sixty was found at Boot Canyon on November 4, 1967 (Wauer). Spring migrants begin to move into the area during the second week of March, and they become fairly common until mid-April. There is a lapse of sightings for a couple of weeks, followed by numerous sightings again from the last of April to May 25. There is also a single June sighting of three birds in the Basin on June 10, 1968 (Wauer).

LESSER GOLDFINCH. *Spinus psaltria*

Fairly common summer and winter resident. This is the common goldfinch of the Big Bend area. Although it can usually be found in the mountains and along the river any time of the year, it is most numerous in the mountains in summer and along the river in winter. Nesting occurs from May through September. It prefers areas of broadleaf trees and shrubs but can be found on conifers as well. I have found singing males among the Arizona Cypress in Boot Canyon during the second week of August in 1968 and 1969.

RED CROSSBILL. *Loxia curvirostra*

Sporadic visitor to the Chisos woodlands. This highland species was first reported for the Chisos Mountains by Oberholser, who found it there in June, 1901, and considered it to be a probable breeding species. Although it may nest during wet years or invasion years, I have found no evidence of nesting in five years. One or two sightings are reported almost every year, and some years this species is common. The winter of 1967–68 was apparently an invasion year, because the Red Crossbill was abundant in the Chisos from August 13 through June 11. I found twelve birds foraging on pinyons at Laguna Meadow on November 15, four along the East Rim on January 28, twelve near the Pinnacles on May 3, and forty near Boot Springs on May 25. A specimen taken on May 3 represents the *benti* race of birds that breeds in the Rocky Mountains from northern New Mexico to Utah and Montana.

GREEN-TAILED TOWHEE. *Chlorura chlorura*

Fairly common migrant and winter resident, and Tarleton Smith reported a nest containing eggs from 4,500 feet in the Chisos Basin on July 10, 1936. The only other evidence of nesting is that of an apparently territorial bird seen above Laguna Meadow, May 28, 1971, by Parker and Murrin. The bird reaches the Big Bend area as early as September 19 in fall but does not become common until mid-October, when it may be numerous along the arroyos below 5,000 feet elevation. Fall migration subsides by early November, but stragglers and winter residents can usually be found at thickets almost everywhere below the pinyon-juniper-oak woodlands.

It can most easily be found at the Old Ranch and Dugout Wells, although it is also present throughout winter and spring along the floodplain and at washes near Panther Junction. The population begins to increase about mid-March as northbound birds enter the area. The spring migration, usually greater than the fall movement, reaches a peak during the second week of April. There is a slight lapse in sightings during mid-April, followed by another increase from April 24 to May 6, and stragglers continue to pass through the area until May 17.

RUFOUS-SIDED TOWHEE. *Pipilo erythrophthalmus*

Fairly common permanent resident in the mountains, and uncommon migrant and winter resident elsewhere. Nesting birds are confined to the wooded canyons of the Chisos and nest during May, June, July, and August. The majority seem to remain on their breeding territories throughout the year; one banded at Boot Springs on January 26 was recaptured there again on May 7. Some fall dispersal is evident in September, when high-country birds apparently move into the lower canyons. Fall migrants have not been recorded until the middle of October; the earliest sighting along the river is one at Rio Grande Village on October 18. This bird then becomes regular at localized places throughout the winter. Spring migrants come to the Big Bend area by mid-March, reach a peak during the second week of April, and have been recorded only once after April 21, one at Rio Grande Village on May 15, 1968 (Wauer).

BROWN TOWHEE. *Pipilo fuscus*

Abundant resident of the Sotol-grasslands and less numerous in the higher mountains and within the lower arroyos. This is the plain brown bird that is numerous in the Basin Campground and around the cottages. Nesting occurs from April throughout the summer and fall during wet years; in 1966 I found an adult bird feeding a spotted youngster on the Lost Mine Trail on November 6. Apparently, there is some altitudinal movement during some winters; it was recorded at Rio Grande Village from September 21 through April in 1969–70, but I have not found it there during other winters.

LARK BUNTING. *Calamospiza melanocorys*

Fairly common migrant and sporadic winter visitor. There is a lapse of records only from May 29 to August 3. Fall migrants may reach the park area as early as August 4. They do not become regular until early September, and a peak is reached during the middle of the month. Migrants continue to trickle through the area until October 18. With some searching, wintering birds can usually be found around Panther Junction, Rio Grande Village, and the Castolon area. Some winters it may be abundant, and flocks of 100 or more birds are not uncommon: 252 were banded at Panther Junction during the 1967–68 winter, none in 1968–69, 23 in 1969–70, and 52 in 1970–71. Wintering birds, as well as migrants, remain below 4,500 feet elevation; there are no records for the Basin. Spring migration starts about March 6, and from March 17 to May 7 it may be numerous along the river and in desert washes. On March 22 and 23, 1969, thousands of Lark Buntings were seen moving along the river between Boquillas and Stillwell Crossing (Wauer). Stragglers may be seen as late as May 28.

SAVANNAH SPARROW. *Passerculus sandwichensis*

Uncommon migrant and winter visitor. Early fall migrants may reach the park by September 14, but this bird is most numerous during the latter part of October. Wintering birds can usually be found at weedy patches and grassy flats along the river and in the lower washes up to 4,500 feet elevation. Spring migrants begin to move through the area by mid-March and may be quite numerous along the river. The latest sighting is at Rio Grande Village on May 24, 1967. At least two different races of Savannah Sparrows visit the park. They look considerably different, and this variation can lead to confusion; the wintering resident and early spring migrant is smaller and lighter than the large, dark form, which is a migrant only.

GRASSHOPPER SPARROW. *Ammodramus savannarum*

Uncommon migrant in spring and rare in fall, and sporadic winter resident at grassy areas from the floodplain to the lower mountain canyons. It has been recorded as early as September 26, but southbound birds cannot be expected with regularity. During the winter of 1967–68 this bird was present at weedy places in Green Gulch and in Panther Canyon, as well as in old fields at Castolon, from December 5 through March 19, but I could not find it at these localities the next two winters. Spring migrants pass through the park area from March 8 to April 4, and except for a lone bird in the Basin on May 18, 1967 (Wauer), sightings are all below 5,000 feet.

BAIRD'S SPARROW. *Ammodramus bairdii*

Rare migrant and sporadic winter visitor. Records range from September 6 through January 25, and from April 2 to May 21. All sightings are from weedy areas below 4,000 feet elevation. I have found it regularly only from mid-October to late December at old fields near Castolon and at Rio Grande Village. The most productive places have been along the Santa Elena Crossing roadway and adjacent to Alamo Creek near the paved Santa Elena Canyon road.

LE CONTE'S SPARROW. *Passerherbulus caudacutus*

There are but four records of this sparrow; three at Rio Grande Village: the Bedells saw two individuals on March 10, 1963, and I found one on August 29 and two on October 29, 1966. Ben Feltner found one in open fields at Castolon, January 3, 1972.

VESPER SPARROW. *Pooecetes gramineus*

Common migrant and fairly common winter resident. Fall

migrants reach the area as early as August 27 and become common from mid-September through October. Migrants can usually be found along the roadways and at weedy places almost everywhere below 5,400 feet, although this sparrow may be expected in the highlands as well; I found several near the East Rim on September 25, 1967. Wintering birds are generally restricted to the lower, weedy flats and seem to be somewhat sporadic in occurrence. I have found Vespers most numerous during certain "sparrow" winters, such as 1967–68, when twenty-four individuals were banded at Panther Junction between January 13 and April 18. During that period, except for Chippers, it was the most numerous sparrow banded. Spring migrants reach the park by mid-March; there is a peak in sightings during the first two weeks of April, progressively declining until May 17.

LARK SPARROW. *Chondestes grammacus*

Fairly common migrant and uncommon post-nesting visitor. This is a common nesting bird at weedy thickets along roadsides and washes of northern Brewster County. It may nest in similar places within the park; I found a lone bird at Panther Junction on June 6, 1967, and Easterla saw one at Ernst Tinaja on June 29, 1968. Small flocks of three to ten birds begin to move into the area during the last week of July and become regular at old fields and weedy areas from mid-August until October 24; there is a peak in the fall migration from August 19 to mid-September. There are lone November and December sightings; I found lone birds near Solis on November 11, 1967, and at Gano Spring on December 29, 1970. There are no records for January and February, but northbound migrants arrive as early as March 19. Spring migrants are most common from mid-April through May 8, and less numerous thereafter until May 18. There are a few records for the Chisos Basin, but for the most part, this species is pretty well confined to the desert and arroyos below 4,000 feet elevation.

RUFOUS-CROWNED SPARROW. *Aimophila ruficeps*

Common permanent resident of the Sotol-grasslands and less numerous within the pinyon-juniper-oak woodlands and the upper desert arroyos. This species is static in its occurrence; a bird banded at Boot Springs on January 26, 1968, was seen there on February 23 and May 8, 1968, and on June 7, 1970 (Wauer). Nesting occurs during April and May and again during the summer rainy period in July, August, and September. In fact, in the lower part of its range, nesters are much more active during wet summers than in spring. Counters found 47 individuals in 1966, 129 in 1967, 110 in 1968, 16 in 1969, and 83 in 1970 on Chisos Mountains Christmas Counts.

CASSIN'S SPARROW. *Aimophila cassinii*

Common summer resident in wet years (but it may be completely absent during dry years), fairly common migrant, and uncommon winter resident. This is one of the Big Bend's most fascinating sparrows because of its almost complete dependence upon the spring and summer rainy season for nesting. It is a regular nesting sparrow of the grasslands in northern Brewster County and north to Fort Stockton and Fort Davis; I have found singing birds along the highways every May, June, and July, and during August and September in wet years. It is a very sporadic nesting bird within the park, however. In 1967, three "skylarking" males were observed in lower Green Gulch on June 3, and fifteen singing birds were counted there on July 30, several days after heavy showers. In 1968, cool and moist weather prevailed from April through September. A few singing birds were heard in Green Gulch as early as June 27, and an estimated thirty-five "skylarking" birds were counted there on July 4. The summer of 1969 was exceptionally dry. Cassin's Sparrows were found singing at a few places in spring, but searches for nesting birds in Green Gulch in June, July, and August proved fruitless, although five to seven individuals were found singing on Dog Canyon Flat on June 6. In 1970, I did not find any singing birds during the relatively dry spring and early summer, but after some rainy periods in July and August the Cassin's Sparrow became the most numerous singing bird of the grassy areas of the park below 4,000 feet. In fact, "skylarking" birds were seen in numbers at Rio Grande Village and along the River Road all during August; I found an estimated thirty singing birds along the River Road on August 21. Most of these birds had left the area by mid-September, but many remained at grassy places throughout the fall and winter.

During drier years, when nesting birds are not already numerous during August and September, there is a distinct movement of migrants into the park during the first week of September. This burst of migrants is over by September 20. Wintering birds can usually be found at choice weedy places along the river, such as old fields at Castolon and Rio Grande Village. A high count of fifty-eight birds was recorded on the Chisos Mountains Christmas Count of December 28, 1968. Singing begins during the second week of March at these wintering areas, but these birds are soon replaced with spring migrants. There are only a few sightings from mid-April to June 25, but this lapse apparently depends solely upon the precipitation, because as soon as the rains begin it is only a few days before singing birds can be found.

BLACK-THROATED SPARROW. *Amphispiza bilineata*

Common permanent resident of the shrub desert and less numerous along the floodplain and up to 4,200 feet elevation in the Sotol-grasslands. Nesting takes place from April to June and again in July, August, and September if the rains produce suitable seed plants. This little sparrow can be found in flocks of five to thirty birds during much of the year and can easily be detected by its tinkling calls. It is somewhat shy during nesting. Youngsters lack the typical black throats of adults. This difference may be confusing, but they almost always are accompanied by adults. Black-throats are the park's most commonly seen desert sparrow.

SAGE SPARROW. *Amphispiza belli*

Sporadic winter visitor only. This western species may be more common within the Big Bend than records indicate. I found a small flock in a grassy area near upper Tornillo Creek bridge on January 5, 1969; thirteen were counted there on January 18, and one of ten seen was collected on February 11. There is one more sighting in 1969: Robert Rothstein found a "few" birds just east of Castolon on March 19. On October 23, 1970, the Wilsons and I found a lone bird at Rio Grande Village, and Tucker and Barlow found three near Nine Point Draw bridge on December 31, 1970.

SLATE-COLORED JUNCO. *Junco hyemalis*

Uncommon migrant and winter resident from October 20 through March 25. It has been recorded from the river floodplain up to Boot Canyon, but the only place I have found it consistently is along the Window Trail between December 1 and March 25. It is almost always seen alone, or with a small flock of Oregons or Gray-heads, but two or three birds are only rarely found together.

OREGON JUNCO. *Junco oreganus*

Fairly common migrant and winter resident in the mountains and less numerous elsewhere. It arrives as early as October 20 and has not been reported after April 6. Most sightings are of one to eight birds along the Window Trail or at Boot Springs, and migrants are often in association with Slate-colored and Gray-headed juncos. Although some ornithologists consider all the dark-eyed juncos as one species, they will be considered separately here because each possesses distinct characteristics.

GRAY-HEADED JUNCO. *Junco caniceps*

Uncommon migrant and fairly common winter resident.

Fall birds may arrive as early as October 9, and the latest spring record is of a flock of approximately twenty-five birds that was seen at Boot Springs on May 27, 1968. This same flock (five were banded) was also recorded on October 22, 1967, February 13 and 23, and March 31, 1968. Three birds of the same flock were recaptured at Boot Springs on October 20, 1968, and the flock remained again until at least May 9. This is the most numerous wintering junco in the mountains.

CHIPPING SPARROW. *Spizella passerina*

Common migrant and fairly common winter visitor. Pansy Espy reports that it nests in the Davis Mountains. This is probably the park's most numerous sparrow from October to mid-May. It has been recorded every month but June. There is a lapse of sightings from May 26 to July 19; a post-nesting bird was caught, banded, and released at Panther Junction on July 19, 1970. It does not become regular in occurrence until late September. The fall movement continues through October and reaches a peak in early October. when mixed flocks of Chippers and Clay-colored Sparrows and a few Brewer's Sparrows are common along the desert roadways and floodplain. Most flocks of *Spizellas* seen in the mountains are almost all Chippers.

Wintering birds are most numerous below 5,500 feet elevation, but they can usually be found among the pinyon-juniper woodlands on the South and East rims during warmer winter days. Chippers can always be found in winter near the sewage lagoons in the Basin, and small flocks are fairly common on the floodplain. Spring migration is well underway by the third week of March. Flocks of thirty to fifty birds can often be found feeding under the cottonwoods at Rio Grande Village and Cottonwood Campground and on open ground in the Chisos Basin. The northbound movement does not begin to subside until the middle of May, and stragglers have been recorded through May 25.

CLAY-COLORED SPARROW. *Spizella pallida*

Sporadic migrant and winter resident. Some years this bird is almost as numerous as the Chipping Sparrow, and other years it is rare. Records range from September 3 through May 31 and are almost totally confined to the open desert and arroyos below 4,000 feet elevation; I have found it in the mountain woodlands only a few times. In September, 1968, it was abundant; only one was seen at Dugout Wells on September 10, but on the morning of September 17, thousands were found over the desert. These birds were in the company of Lark Buntings and an occasional Field or Lincoln's sparrow. This wave of sparrows subsided by late afternoon, and I found only a few individuals in the same area on September 19. The winters of 1968–69 and 1970–71 were good "sparrow" winters, and Clay-colors could be found at weedy fields along the river all winter. Northbound migrants begin to move into the area by mid-March and a peak is reached during the first week of April. Stragglers continue to pass through the park until May 4. During the 1969–70 fall, winter, and spring, the bird was recorded from September 19 through October 26, none were seen during November, December, January, and February, and only a few migrants were recorded from March 18 to May 6.

BREWER'S SPARROW. *Spizella breweri*

Uncommon migrant and sporadic winter visitor. Records range from October 20 through May 6. Like the Clay-colored Sparrow, the Brewer's rarely is seen above 4,500 feet elevation. Fall migrants are somewhat sporadic and are almost always in association with Chippers or Clay-colored Sparrows. Wintering birds can be found at weedy fields along the river during "sparrow" years; I found it during the winters of 1966–67, 1968–69, and 1970–71 at Rio Grande Village and Castolon. It was present within the Sotol-grassland all winter of 1970–71, as well. During the spring migration it can be found with certainty only from mid-March through mid-April. A peak is reached from March 15 to 27, and flocks of ten to fifty birds can often be detected by their chorus of musical trills. Stragglers may be found in the park until May 6.

FIELD SPARROW. *Spizella pusilla*

Sporadic migrant and winter visitor. Like the rest of the *Spizellas*, this little sparrow may be fairly common during some winters and hard to find other winters. During 1967–68 it was found in numbers throughout the grassy slopes of the Chisos below 5,000 feet elevation. A specimen was taken at Rio Grande Village on November 19, and nine individuals were banded at Panther Junction on the following dates: December 31, January 10 (two) and 15, February 3, 6, and 27, and March 15 and 17. In 1968–69, several were found along the river and in the grasslands from September 15 to March 15. But I found only one during the entire fall, winter, and spring of 1969–70, at Castolon on December 21. It was present in small numbers up to 4,000 feet throughout the 1970–71 winter.

BLACK-CHINNED SPARROW. *Spizella atrogularis*

Fairly common summer resident at chaparral areas above 5,200 feet, and sporadic winter resident. Singing birds have been recorded as early as March 17 in the Basin, where the Black-chin can often be found along the upper part of the Window Trail and adjacent to the campground. It nests there, along the north and west slopes below Casa Grande, and on the northern slope below Laguna Meadow adjacent to the South Rim Trail. Some years it is abundant at Laguna Meadow; twelve singing birds were counted on the chaparral flat there on May 7, 1970. During dry years it apparently waits until the summer rainy season before nesting. In 1969, except for eight to ten singing birds heard along the north slope of Blue Creek Canyon on April 5, I was able to find singing birds only above Boot Canyon (7,100 feet elevation) on June 10, and another carrying nesting materials at Laguna Meadow on July 20.

Wintering Black-chins may be fairly common at weedy patches in the canyons between 4,400 and 5,400 feet elevation, but some winters they are difficult or impossible to find. In 1967, fifteen were found in Pulliam Canyon on January 20, and twelve along the Window Trail on January 21. There is a defined downward movement in winter; none have been recorded above 5,400 feet from November 6 through mid-April. If enough rain falls during summer to produce a good grass crop, the Black-chin can usually be found wintering along the Window Trail (just below the sewage lagoons is a good place), along the edge of the upper Basin (near the Chisos Trailhead), and at weedy patches in middle Green Gulch.

HARRIS' SPARROW. *Zonotrichia querula*

There are but three records of this large sparrow for the park. The Hurlberts saw one at the Santa Elena Canyon picnic area on February 25, 1965; the Bedells recorded one at Rio Grande Village from February 15 to 22, 1966; and a lone adult visited my feeder at Panther Junction from November 30 to December 6, 1968. It was captured, photographed, banded, and released.

WHITE-CROWNED SPARROW. *Zonotrichia leucophrys*

Common migrant and winter resident below 5,000 feet elevation. It has been recorded from September 15 through June 4. Early fall migrants are restricted to the Rio Grande Valley and do not appear in the higher elevations until mid-October, when it may be common along the river, uncommon in the grasslands, but rare in the lower woodlands. Wintering birds are common all along the river but sporadic at higher elevations. During the 1966–67 winter, I banded 472 White-crowns at Panther Junction, but only 112 in 1967–68, 105 in 1968–69, none in 1969–70, and 22 in 1970–71. This

species is most numerous at Rio Grande Village and Cottonwood Campground, where wintering birds may remain until
late May. Spring migrants begin to move through the park
area by mid-March and may be numerous along the floodplain and at adjacent mesquite bosques until mid-May. Stragglers may pass through the lowlands until June.

GOLDEN-CROWNED SPARROW. *Zonotrichia atricapilla*

There are but three sightings of at least two birds. An immature bird was captured (and banded) with a flock of several hundred White-crowns in Alamo Creek near Castolon,
on December 9, 1971 (Wauer). I found it there again on
December 28, and Ben Feltner observed an unbanded
juvenal there on January 3, 1972.

WHITE-THROATED SPARROW. *Zonotrichia albicollis*

Uncommon winter visitor and migrant from November 2
through May 10. Although this species is never numerous,
it occurs regularly at lowland, brushy areas during winter. I
have found it most often near riparian habitats along the
river, and less numerous at higher areas, such as Dugout
Wells, Grapevine, and the Old Ranch. It also occurs irregularly in the lower mountain canyons, such as lower Green
Gulch, and along the Window Trail. In migration it can be
expected anywhere below 5,000 feet. Two birds were seen
at my feeder at Panther Junction during a snowstorm on
March 21, 1967.

FOX SPARROW. *Passerella iliaca*

Rare winter visitor. John Galley first reported this bird for
the park when he found a lone individual at the Santa Elena
Canyon picnic area on February 1, 1967. A specimen, ap-
parently the same individual, was taken at this locality on
February 12, 1967, and proved to be the eastern race *zaboria*
(Wauer, 1969*b*). I have since seen it only three times in sim-
ilar habitats, near Rio Grande Village on November 1 and
December 17, 1967, and December 23, 1970.

LINCOLN'S SPARROW. *Melospiza lincolnii*

Common migrant in spring, and fairly common in fall and winter. This perky little sparrow has been recorded within the park as early as September 15 and as late as May 25. Fall migrants reach a peak from October 19 to 26, but they can usually be found at weedy patches along the river and in canyons to 5,300 feet almost any time during migration and in winter. Spring migrants become numerous from March 15 to April 11, and stragglers continue to pass through the area until late May.

SWAMP SPARROW. *Melospiza georgiana*

Uncommon migrant and fairly common winter resident at a few localized water areas along the river. Fall migrants do not reach the Big Bend area until October 5 and have been recorded as late as May 20. This bird is usually more common than the related Song Sparrow, which utilizes the same habitat, and can best be found at the beaver dam area and silt pond at Rio Grande Village. Swamp Sparrows and Yellowthroats can usually be squeaked out of hiding at these places throughout the winter and spring. It also can be found at weedy fields below 4,500 feet elevation during winters following wet summers.

SONG SPARROW. *Melospiza melodia*

Uncommon migrant and rare winter visitor. Fall birds reach the area as early as October 12, a peak is reached from October 25 to 28, and late migrants can usually be found throughout December. This species is rarely seen in January and February, but it can be found with considerable searching at swampy or weedy places along the river. Northbound birds begin to move along the river by the second week of March and become most numerous from April 1 to 11; a high of five birds was seen at Rio Grande Village on April 8, 1970 (Wauer). Stragglers have been recorded within the park until May 10.

CHESTNUT-COLLARED LONGSPUR. *Calcarius ornatus*

Rare spring migrant. It was first reported by Thompson G. Marsh, who found a lone bird atop the South Rim, walking along the trail in front of him, on March 25, 1960. Hurlbert observed one on Tornillo Flat on April 5, 1961. There were no other park records until 1970, when an immature male was taken at my feeder at Panther Junction on March 13, and a group of four individuals was seen there on March 12, 20, 23, and 24. Apparently, this is an irregular spring visitor to the Big Bend area. Van Tyne and Sutton reported a flock of fifteen birds at a stock pond seventeen miles northeast of Marathon on April 4 and 12, 1935. They also found four McCown's Longspurs (*Rhynchophanes mccownii*) on the latter date, a species that should be looked for within the park as well. The two above species, as well as the Smith's Longspur (*Calcarius pictus*) rarely. can usually be found near Lake Balmorhea during more severe winters.

Birds of Uncertain Occurrence

The following list includes a number of birds that are not contained within the regular annotated list, because they need further documentation. In general, this hypothetical list includes those species that have not been authenticated by either a specimen or a sighting by more than one individual or party.

ANHINGA. *Anhinga anhinga*

Wildlife photographer Bert Schaughency and his wife saw one flying over the river at Hot Springs on April 23, 1970. As far as can be determined. this is the first sighting of this species for the Trans-Pecos.

WHITE-TAILED KITE. *Elanus leucurus*

Mr. and Mrs. Robert W. Foster reported watching one of these graceful birds for several minutes over Dog Canyon Flat, April 17, 1971.

PECTORAL SANDPIPER. *Erolia melanotos*

The only park sighting of this shorebird is one reported by Lovie Mae Whitaker for Hot Springs on July 19, 1942.

BLACK TERN. *Chlidonias niger*

There are no park records of this little tern, but it apparently is a rare spring and fall visitor at water areas throughout the Big Bend Country. The Millers recorded it on their ranch on August 23, 1956, May 20, 1957, and August 30, 1965; I observed one just west of Marathon on August 21, 1970; and Scudday collected one of several seen at Lake Balmorhea on September 16, 1970. There also is a single record of a Caspian Tern (*Hydroprogne caspia*); I found a lone bird with the Black Tern west of Marathon on August 21, 1970.

RED-BILLED PIGEON. *Columba flavirostris*

Alexander Sprunt, Jr., and John H. Dick reported seeing two fly over their cottages in the Chisos Basin on July 21, 1951. It was seen "in good light and at low elevation, which revealed characteristics perfectly."

BARRED OWL. *Strix varia*

Mr. and Mrs. Robert Foster reported hearing this eastern owl calling several times within Reagan Canyon, below La Linda on the Rio Grande, during the night of November 25, 1971.

BLACK SWIFT. *Cypseloides niger*

There is a single sighting of this large swift for the Trans-Pecos. Alexander Sprunt, Jr., and John Dick reported "five or six individuals" from the South Rim Trail over Blue Creek Canyon on July 22, 1951.

COPPERY-TAILED TROGON. *Trogon elegans*

There is but one sighting of this beautiful bird. Sue Corson saw a lone male in the trees near the Chisos Basin sewage lagoons on May 9, 1969. She watched it for several minutes through binoculars. Although this species will remain hypothetical until it has been recorded again, it is difficult to misidentify a trogon.

HAIRY WOODPECKER. *Dendrocopos villosus*

Brodrick (1960) included this bird on his park listing, based upon a reported sighting at an unknown site on March 10, 1950.

DOWNY WOODPECKER. *Dendrocopos pubescens*

Doyle and Helen Peckham reported seeing this little woodpecker at Rio Grande Village Campground on May 17, 1969.

ROSE-THROATED BECARD. *Platypsaris aglaiae*

Richard B. Starr reported seeing three males and two females in a flock at the Santa Elena Canyon picnic site on September 24, 1965.

KISKADEE FLYCATCHER. *Pitangus sulphuratus*

There is a single sighting for the area; Roy and Jean Hudson reported one along the river at Boquillas on May 21, 1964.

BUFF-BREASTED FLYCATCHER. *Empidonax fulvifrons*

This little flycatcher was reported from near the Chisos Remuda in the Basin by Dr. and Mrs. R. C. Smith, August 12, 1969.

STELLER'S JAY. *Cyanocitta stelleri*

There is but one sighting of this mountain jay for the park: Mrs. Campbell Steketee reported one at the South Rim on March 16, 1970. This crested jay is resident in the Pine and Livermore peaks area of the Davis Mountains, but it does not reside in the Chisos or south in Coahuila's del Carmen Mountains.

COMMON CROW. *Corvus brachyrhynchos*

Barbara Ribble reported seeing two crows flying over Castolon on December 27, 1970.

VEERY. *Hylocichla fuscescens*

This thrush has been reported on three occasions: George R. Shier reported one from Rio Grande Village on March 18 and one from Castolon on March 19, 1969; Byron Griffen reported one from Boot Canyon on May 3, 1970.

CAPE MAY WARBLER. *Dendroica tigrina*

Charles T. Meyer and Michael D. Stuart reported a lone bird at Government Spring on May 19, 1969.

YELLOW-THROATED WARBLER. *Dendroica dominica*

There is one park record of this warbler: Robert H. Glazier, Douglas Zabel, and Eugene R. Lewis observed one at Rio Grande Village on March 31, 1970.

OLIVE-BACKED WARBLER. *Parula pitiayumi*

I found a lone bird in heavy vegetation at the Boquillas Crossing, March 19, 1967, that I believed to be this species.

GOLDEN-CHEEKED WARBLER. *Dendroica chrysoparia*

Fred Gehlbach and his students reported a singing male in upper Boot Canyon on April 9, 1968.

PINE WARBLER. *Dendroica pinus*

David T. Brown and members of the San Antonio Audubon Society reported seeing this bird at Boot Springs on April 27, 1966.

RED-FACED WARBLER. *Cardellina rubrifrons*

Bruce A. Mack reported seeing a lone bird foraging in the trees at Boot Springs on June 5, 1964.

PINE GROSBEAK. *Pinicola enucleator*

Clara and Harold Spore reported seeing one of this northern species in Green Gulch on April 24, 1951.

EVENING GROSBEAK. *Hesperiphona vespertina*

Karl Haller reported this species in the Chisos Basin on the December 30, 1951, Christmas Count.

PURPLE FINCH. *Carpodacus purpureus*

There is a single sighting of two singing males and one female at Rio Grande Village on April 13, 1972, by P. Phillips and J. Greenberg.

MEXICAN JUNCO. *Junco phaeonotus*

There is a lone undated sighting along the Window Trail (National Park Service files). This is a common breeding bird in the del Carmen Mountains of Mexico, fifty miles to the southeast, and post-nesting visitors should be expected.

BIBLIOGRAPHY

American Ornithologists' Union. 1957. *Check-list of North American Birds.* 5th ed. Baltimore, Md.

Arnold, Keith A. 1968. Olivaceous Flycatcher in the Davis Mountains of Texas. *Bull. of the Texas Ornithological Soc.* 2:28.

Bailey, Vernon. 1905. *Biological Survey of Texas.* North Amer. Fauna, no. 25. Washington, D.C.

Barlow, Jon C. 1967. Nesting of the Black-capped Vireo in the Chisos Mountains, Texas. *Condor* 69:605–606.

———, and Roy Johnson. 1967. Current Status of the Elf Owl in the Southwestern United States. *Southwestern Naturalist* 12:331–332.

———, and Roland H. Wauer. 1971. The Gray Vireo (*Vireo vicinior* Coues; Aves: Vireonidae) Wintering in the Big Bend Region, West Texas. *Canadian Jour. Zool.* 49:953–955.

Blair, W. Frank. 1950. The Biotic Provinces of Texas. *Texas Journal of Science* 2:93–116.

Blake, Emmet R. 1953. *Birds of Mexico.* Chicago: University of Chicago Press.

Borell, Adrey E. 1936. Birds Observed in the Big Bend Area of Brewster County, Texas. Typewritten report to National Park Service.

———. 1938. New Bird Records for Brewster County, Texas. *Condor* 40:181–182.

Brandt, Herbert W. 1938. Two New Birds from the Chisos Mountains, Texas. *Auk* 55:269–270.

———. 1940. *Texas Bird Adventures.* Cleveland: Bird Research Foundation.

Brodkorb, Pierce. 1935. A New Flycatcher from Texas. *Occ. Papers, Mus. Zool., Univ. Mich.,* no. 306.

Brodrick, Harold. 1960. Check-list of the Birds of Big Bend National Park. Mimeographed. Big Bend National Park.

————; C. Philip Allen; and Anne LeSassier. 1966. *Checklist of Birds of Big Bend National Park*. Big Bend National Park, Texas: Big Bend Natural History Association.

Correll, Donovan S., and Marshall C. Johnston. 1970. *Manual of Vascular Plants of Texas*. Renner, Texas: Texas Research Foundation.

Cottam, Clarence, and J. B. Trefethen, eds. 1968. *Whitewings: The Life History, Status and Management of the Whitewing Dove*. New York: D. Van Nostrand Co.

Cruickshank, Allen. 1950. Records from Brewster County, Texas. *Wilson Bull*. 62:217–219.

Dixon, Keith L. 1959. Ecological and Distributional Relations of Desert Scrub Birds of Western Texas. *Condor* 61:397–409.

————, and O. C. Wallmo. 1956. Some New Bird Records from Brewster County, Texas. *Condor* 58:166.

Ely, Charles A. 1962. The Birds of Southeastern Coahuila, Mexico. *Condor* 64:34–39.

Espy, Pansy. 1969. Birds of the Davis Mountains: The Phalarope. Mimeographed by Midland Naturalist, Midland, Texas, September.

Freidmann, Herbert; L. Griscom; and R. T. Moore. 1957. Distributional Check-list of the Birds of Mexico, Part II. *Pacific Coast Avifauna* 33:1–435.

Fuertes, Louis Agassiz. 1903. With the Mearns Quail in Southwestern Texas. *Condor* 5:113–116.

Galley, John E. 1951. Clark's Nutcracker in the Chisos Mountains, Texas. *Wilson Bull*. 62:188.

Hubbard, John P. 1969. The Relationships and Evolution of the Dendroica cornota Complex. *Auk* 86:393–432.

McBee, Lena G., and Mary Belle Keefer. 1967. Field Checklist of Birds—Region of El Paso, Texas. El Paso Audubon Soc.

Marshall, Joe T., Jr. 1967. *Parallel Variation in North and Middle American Screech Owls*. Monographs of the Western Foundation of Vertebrate Zoology. Los Angeles, Calif.

Maxon, George E. 1916. Military Oologing in Texas. *Oologist* 33 (10):172–173.

————. 1916. A Soldier Ornithologist. *Oologist* 33(12):205–206.

Miller, Alden H. 1955. The Avifauna of the Sierra del Carmen of Coahuila, Mexico. *Condor* 57:154–178.

Miller, Jody and Clay. 1970. List of Birds seen on the Miller Ranch. Typed list.

Montgomery, Thomas H., Jr. 1905. Summer Resident Birds of Brewster County, Texas. *Auk* 22:12–15.

Nelson, Richard Clay. 1970. An Additional Nesting Record of the Lucifer Hummingbird in the United States. *Southwestern Naturalist* 15:135–136.

Oberholser, Harry C. 1902. Some Notes from Western Texas. *Auk* 19:300–301.

Ohlendorf, Harry F., and Robert F. Patton. 1971. Nesting Record of Mexican Duck (*Anas diazi*) in Texas. *Wilson Bull.* 83:97.

Palmer, Ralph S. 1962. *Handbook of North American Birds*, vol. 1. New Haven: Yale University Press.

Peterson, Roger Tory. 1960. *A Field Guide to the Birds of Texas.* Boston: Houghton Mifflin Company.

Phillips, Allan R. 1968. The Instability of the Distribution of Land Birds in the Southwest. *Paper of the Archeological Soc. of New Mex.* 1:129–162.

————; Joe Marshall; and Gale Monson. 1964. *The Birds of Arizona.* Tucson: Univ. of Arizona Press.

Pulich, Warren M., Sr., and Warren M. Pulich, Jr. 1963. The Nesting of the Lucifer Hummingbird in the United States. *Auk* 80: 370–371.

Quillin, Roy W. 1935. New Bird Records from Texas. *Auk* 52:324–325.

Raitt, Ralph J. 1967. Relationship between Black-eared and Plain-eared Forms of Bushtits (*Psaltriparus*). *Auk* 84:503–528.

Rooney, Walter. 1966. Taped interview by Doug Evans for National Park Service.

Selander, Robert K., and Donald R. Giller. 1961. Analysis of sympatry of Great-tailed and Boat-tailed grackles. *Condor* 63:29–86.

Smith, Austin Paul. 1917. Some Birds of the Davis Mountains, Texas. *Condor* 19:161–165.

Smith, Tarleton F. 1936. Wildlife Report on the Proposed Big Bend National Park of Texas. Typewritten report for National Park Service, October 11.

Sprunt, Alexander, Jr. 1950. The Colima Warbler of the Big Bend. *Audubon Magazine* 52:84–91.

Stevenson, John O. 1935. General Wildlife Considerations of the Big Bend Area of Texas. Typewritten report to National Park Service.

_____, and Tarleton F. Smith. 1938. Additions to the Brewster County, Texas, Bird List. *Condor* 40:184.

Stine, Doug. 1966. The Birds of Balmorhea Lake. Typewritten report, Sul Ross State College, May 10.

Sutton, George M. 1935. An Expedition to the Big Bend Country. *The Cardinal* 4:1–7.

_____. 1936. *Birds in the Wilderness*. New York: MacMillan Co.

_____. 1951. *Mexican Birds—First Impressions*. Norman: Univ. of Oklahoma Press.

_____, and Josselyn Van Tyne. 1935. A New Red-tailed Hawk from Texas. *Occ. Papers, Mus. Zool., Univ. Mich.*, no. 321, September 23.

Taylor, Walter P.; W. B. McDougall; and W. B. Davis. 1944. Preliminary Report of an Ecological Survey of Big Bend National Park. Mimeographed report to National Park Service, March–June.

Thompson, Ben H. 1934. Report upon the Wildlife of the Big Bend Area of the Rio Grande, Texas. Typewritten report to National Park Service, April 18.

Thompson, William Lay. 1953. The Ecological Distribution of the Birds of the Black Gap Area, Brewster County, Texas. *Texas Jour. Sci.* 2:158–177.

Van Tyne, Josselyn. 1929. Notes on Some Birds of the Chisos Mountains of Texas. *Auk* 46:204–206.

_____. 1936. The Discovery of the Nest of the Colima Warbler (*Vermivora crissalis*). *Univ. of Michigan, Miscellaneous Publications*, no. 33.

_____, and George M. Sutton. 1937. The Birds of Brewster County, Texas. *Univ. of Michigan Press, Miscellaneous Publications*, no. 37.

Wauer, Roland H. 1967a. Report on the Colima Warbler Census. Mimeographed report to National Park Service, May 29.

_____. 1967b. Winter and Early Spring Birds in Big Bend. *Bull. of Texas Ornithological Soc.* 1 (1):8.

_____. 1967c. Further Evidence of Bushtit Lumping in Texas. *Bull. of Texas Ornithological Soc.* 1 (5–6):1.

_____. 1967d. Colima Warbler Census in Big Bend's Chisos Mountains. *National Parks Magazine* 41:8–10.

_____. 1967e. First Thick-billed Kingbird Record for Texas. *Southwestern Naturalist* 12:485–486.

_____. 1968a. *Checklist of the Birds of Big Bend National Park*.

Big Bend National Park, Texas: Big Bend Natural History Association.

————. 1968*b*. The Groove-billed Ani in Texas. *Southwestern Naturalist* 13:452.

————. 1969*a*. Hummingbirds of the Big Bend. *Bull. of Texas Ornithologist Soc.* 3:18.

————. 1969*b*. Winter Bird Records from the Chisos Mountains and Vicinity. *Southwestern Naturalist* 14:252–254.

————. 1969*c*. The History of Land Use and Some Ecological Implications, Big Bend National Park, Texas. Typewritten report to National Park Service, November 25.

————. 1970*a*. Upland Plover at Big Bend National Park, Texas. *Southwestern Naturalist* 14:361–362.

————. 1970*b*. The Occurrence of the Black-vented Oriole, *Icterus wagleri*, in the United States. *Auk* 87:811–812.

————. 1970*c*. A Second Swallow-tailed Kite Record for Trans-Pecos, Texas. *Wilson Bull.* 82:462.

————. 1971. The Ecological Distribution of Birds of the Chisos Mountains, Texas. *Southwestern Naturalist* 16:1–29.

————, and M. Kent Rylander. 1968. Anna's Hummingbird in West Texas. *Auk* 85:501.

Wolfe, Col. L. R. 1956. *Checklist of the Birds of Texas*. Personal publication.

INDEX

Page numbers for major annotations are in italics. Pages on which illustrations occur are enclosed by parentheses.

Anhinga, *205*
Ani
 Groove-billed, 35, *97*
Avocet
 American, *90*

Becard
 Rose-throated, *207*
Bittern
 American, 35, *60*
 Least, *60*
Blackbird
 Brewer's, 35, 52, 170, *177*, 179
 Redwinged, *170*
 Rusty, 52, 63, *176*
 Yellow-headed, *169*, 170
Bluebird
 Eastern, 52, *140*
 Mountain, 52, *141*
 Western, 52, *141*
Bufflehead, 52, *67*
Bunting
 Indigo, 36, *185*
 Lark, 40, 52, *192*, 199
 Lazuli, *185*
 Painted, 12, 31, 36, 40, (41), 42, 178, 185, *187*
 Varied, (44), 45, 52, *185*
Bushtit, 36, 45, (46), 49, 50, 52, *129*

Canvasback, 52, *66*
Caracara, *77*

Cardinal, 36, 40, (41), 51, *182*
Catbird, 12, *135*
Chat
 Yellow-breasted, 12, 35, 40, (41), 42, *164*, 176, 178
Chuckar, *82*
Coot
 American, 35, 42, 52, *85*
Cormorant
 Olivaceous, *56*
Cowbird
 Bronzed, 170, 171, *179*
 Brown-headed, 36, 40, 45, 49, 157, 177, *178*
Crane
 Sandhill, *82*
Creeper
 Brown, 50, 52, *131*
Crossbill
 Red, 50, *190*
Crow
 Common, *208*
Cuckoo
 Yellow-billed, 12, 35, 40, (41), 42, *96*
Curlew
 Long-billed, *86*

Dickcissel, 36, *187*
Dove
 Ground, 35, 52, *95*
 Inca, 35, *95*
 Mourning, 35, 40, 42, 45, 49, 51, *94*

Rock, *93*
White-fronted, *95*
White-winged, 35, 40, (41), 42,
    45, 49, 51, *93*
Dowitcher
    Long-billed, *90*
Duck
    Black, *63*
    Mexican, *63*
    Ring-necked, 52, *66*
    Ruddy, *67*
    Wood, 52, *66*

Eagle
    Bald, *76*
    Golden, 42, 52, *75*
Egret
    Cattle, *58*
    Common, *58*
    Snowy, *59*

Falcon
    Aplomado, *79*
    Peregrine, 42, *78*
    Prairie, 42, 52, *78*
Finch
    Cassin's, 50, 52, *188*
    House, 12, 36, 40, 42, 45, (48),
        49, 51, *188*
    Purple, *209*
Flicker
    Red-shafted, (47), 50, 51, *111*
    Yellow-shafted, 52, *110*
Flycatcher
    Ash-throated, 12, 35, 40, 42,
        (43), 45, 49, 50, 52, *116*
    Buff-breasted, *207*
    Coues', *120*
    Dusky, 36, 50, 52, *119*
    Gray, 36, *119*
    Great Crested, *116*
    Hammond's, 36, *119*
    Kiskadee, *207*
    Least, *119*
    Olivaceous, *117*
    Olive-sided, 35, *121*
    Scissor-tailed, *115*
    Sulphur-bellied, *115*
    Traill's, *118*

Vermilion, 35, (48), 52, *121*
Western, (47), 50, *120*
Wied's Crested, 12, *116*
Yellow-bellied, *118*

Gadwall, 35, 52, 63, *64*
Gallinule
    Common, 35, *84*
    Purple, *84*
Gnatcatcher
    Black-tailed, 12, 35, 40, 42, (43),
        45, 49, 51, *143*, 178
    Blue-gray, 36, 45, (46), 50, 52,
        142, 143
Goldeneye
    Common, *67*
Goldfinch
    American, *189*
    Lesser, 36, 42, 45, 49, 51, *189*
Goose
    Canada, *61*
    Ross', 62
    Snow, *62*
    White-fronted, *62*
Goshawk, *70*
Grackle
    Boat-tailed, 178
    Great-tailed, 52, *177*
Grebe
    Eared, 52, *54*
    Least, 35, 52, *55*
    Pied-billed, 35, 42, 55, 85
Grosbeak
    Black-headed, 45, (47), 49, 50,
        183, 184
    Blue, 12, 36, 40, 42, 45, 178, *184*
    Evening, *209*
    Pine, *209*
    Rose-breasted, *183*
Gull
    Franklin's, *92*
    Laughing, *91*
    Ring-billed, *91*

Hawk
    Black, 12, *75*
    Broad-winged, *72*
    Cooper's, 51, *71*
    Ferruginous, 52, *74*

Gray, *74*
Harris', 52, *74*
Marsh, 52, *76*
Pigeon, *79*
Red-shouldered, *72*
Red-tailed, 35, 42, 49, 51, *71*, *76*
Rough-legged, *74*
Sharp-shinned, 35, 50, 51, *71*
Sparrow, 35, 42, 45, 49, 51, *80*
Swainson's, *72*
White-tailed, *73*
Zone-tailed, 42, 49, *73*
Heron
Great Blue, 52, *56*
Green, 12, 52, *57*
Little Blue, *58*
Louisiana, *59*
Hummingbird
Allen's, *107*
Anna's, 52, *106*
Black-chinned, 34, 35, 40, 45, 49, *105*
Blue-throated, 36, 45, 50, *108*
Broad-billed, *109*
Broad-tailed, 49, 50, 52, *106*
Calliope, *108*
Costa's, *105*
Lucifer, (frontispiece), xv, 34, *103*
Rivoli's, *108*, 109
Ruby-throated, *104*
Rufous, 36, 52, *107*
White-eared, *109*

Ibis
White, *61*
White-faced, *60*
Wood, 60

Jay
Blue, *126*
Mexican, 36, 45, (46), 49, 50, 52, *126*
Pinyon, *128*
Scrub, 52, *126*, 127
Steller's, 127, *207*
Junco
Gray-headed, 36, 52, *197*
Mexican, *209*

Oregon, 52, *197*
Slate-colored, 51, *197*

Killdeer, 35, 39, 42, 51, *85*
Kingbird
Cassin's, *114*
Eastern, *113*
Thick-billed, 52, *115*
Tropical, *113*
Western, 35, *114*
Kingfisher
Belted, 52, *109*
Green, *110*
Ringed, 110
Kinglet
Golden-crowned, 52, *143*
Ruby-crowned, 35, (48), 51, *144*, 159
Kite
Mississippi, *70*
Swallow-tailed, *69*
White-tailed, *205*
Knot, *89*

Lark
Horned, 52, *122*
Longspur
Chestnut-collared, *204*
McCown's, 204
Smith's, 204
Loon
Arctic, 54
Common, 54
Red-throated, 54

Mallard, 52, *63*
Martin
Purple, *125*
Meadowlark
Eastern, *168*
Western, *168*
Merganser
Common, *68*
Hooded, *68*
Red-breasted, 68
Mockingbird, 12, 35, 40, 42, (43), 45, 51, *135*, 175

Nighthawk
Common, *102*

Lesser, 12, 35, 42, (43), *102*
Night Heron
  Black-crowned, *59*
  Yellow-crowned, *59*
Nutcracker
  Clark's, *128*
Nuthatch
  Pygmy, 50, *131*
  Red-breasted, 50, 52, *130*
  White-breasted, xi, 28, (47), 49,
    50, 52, *130*, 159

Oriole
  Baltimore, *173*
  Black-vented, 35, *173*
  Bullock's, *173*
  Hooded, 35, 40, *171*, 172, 174,
    175, 179, 180
  Orchard, 35, 40, *170*, 171, 172,
    175, 176, 180
  Scott's, 35, (44), 45, 49, 52, *172*,
    176, 179
  Wagler's, *173*
Osprey, *77*
Ovenbird, *162*
Owl
  Barn, *97*
  Barred, *206*
  Burrowing, *100*
  Elf, 40, 42, (44), 45, 49, *99*
  Flammulated, (47), 50, *98*
  Great Horned, 35, 42, 49, 51, *99*
  Long-eared, 52, *100*
  Pygmy, *99*
  Saw-whet, *101*
  Screech, 40, 42, 49, 51, *98*
  Short-eared, *101*

Pelican
  Brown, 56
  White, *56*
Pewee
  Western Wood, 35, *120*
Phainopepla, 52, *145*
Phalarope
  Northern, 91
  Wilson's, *91*
Phoebe
  Black, 40, (41), 51, *117*

Eastern, (48), 51, *117*
  Say's, 35, 42, 45, 51, *118*
Pigeon
  Band-tailed, 28, (47), 49, 50, 52,
    92
  Red-billed, *206*
Pintail, 52, *64*
Pipit
  Sprague's, *144*
  Water, 35, 52, *144*, 145
Plover
  Mountain, 85
  Semipalmated, *85*
  Snowy, 85
  Upland, 87
Poor-will, 45, *102*
Pyrrhuloxia, 12, 36, 40, 42, (44),
  45, 51, *183*

Quail
  Blue, 81
  Gambel's, *81*
  Harlequin, *81*
  Mearn's, 82
  Scaled, 36, 42, (43), 45, 51, *80*

Rail
  King, *83*
  Virginia, *83*
Raven
  Common, 35, 42, 45, 51, *127*
  White-necked, *127*
Redhead, *66*
Redstart
  American, 35, *165*
  Painted, *166*
Roadrunner, 35, 40, 42, (43), 45,
  51, *96*
Robin
  American, 51, *138*
  Rufous-backed, *139*

Sandpiper
  Baird's, 39, *89*
  Least, 39, 52, *89*
  Pectoral, *206*
  Solitary, 35, 39, *88*
  Spotted, 35, 39, 51, *87*

Upland, *87*
Western, 52, *90*
Sapsucker
Williamson's, 50, 52, *112*
Yellow-bellied, (48), 51, *112*
Scaup
Lesser, *67*
Shoveler, 35, 52, *65*
Shrike
Loggerhead, (44), 45, 51, *146*
Siskin
Pine, 36, 52, *188*
Snipe
Common, 52, *86*
Solitaire
Townsend's, 31, 52, *142*
Sora, 42, 52, *83*, 85
Sparrow
Baird's, 52, *193*
Black-chinned, 36, (44), 45, 49,
52, *200*
Black-throated, 36, (43), 45, 51,
178, *196*
Brewer's, 36, 51, *199*
Cassin's, 45, 51, *195*
Chipping, 36, 40, 51, 194, *198*
Clay-colored, 36, 198, *199*
Field, 52, *200*
Fox, 52, *202*
Golden-crowned, *202*
Grasshopper, 52, *193*
Harris', *201*
House, 35, 51, *167*, 178
Lark, 36, 40, 52, *194*
Le Conte's, *193*
Lincoln's, 36, 51, *203*
Rufous-crowned, 36, (44), 45, 49,
50, 51, *195*
Sage, *197*
Savannah, 51, *192*
Song, 51, *203*
Swamp, 36, (48), 51, *203*
Vesper, 51, 159, *193*
White-crowned, 36, (48), 51, *201*
White-throated, 52, *202*
Starling, 52, *147*
Stilt
Black-necked, *91*

Stork
Wood, *60*
Swallow
Bank, *123*
Barn, 35, *124*
Cave, *125*
Cliff, 34, (41), 42, *124*, 125, 188
Rough-winged, 35, 51, *123*
Tree, *123*
Violet-green, 34, 35, 45, *122*
Swan
Whistling, 52, *61*
Swift
Black, *206*
Chimney, *103*
White-throated, 35, 42, 45, 49,
52, *103*

Tanager
Hepatic, 45, (46), 49, *181*
Scarlet, *180*
Summer, 36, 40, (41), 42, 45, 49,
181
Western, 36, *180*
Teal
Blue-winged, 35, 52, *64*
Cinnamon, *65*
Green-winged, 35, (48), 52, *64*
Tern
Black, *206*
Caspian, 206
Least, *92*
Thrasher
Brown, 52, *135*
Crissal, 45, 49, 51, *137*
Curve-billed, 35, 51, *136*, 137
Long-billed, *136*
Sage, 52, *137*
Thrush
Gray-cheeked, *140*
Hermit, 35, 51, *139*, 159
Swainson's, *140*
Wood, *139*
Titmouse
Black-crested, 36, 45, (46), 49,
50, 52, *128*
Towhee
Brown, 36, (44), 45, 49, 51, *191*
Green-tailed, 36, 51, *190*

Rufous-sided, 36, (46), 49, 50, 51, 71, *191*
Tree Duck
 Fulvous, *62*
Trogon
 Coppery-tailed, *206*

Veery, *208*
Verdin, 12, 35, 40, 42, (43), 45, 51, *129*
Vireo
 Bell's, 12, 35, 40, (41), 42, *148*, 178
 Black-capped, *147*
 Gray, 36, 45, 49, 52, *149*
 Hutton's, xi, (47), 49, 50, 52, *148*
 Philadelphia, *151*
 Red-eyed, *151*
 Solitary, 35, *150*
 Warbling, 35, *151*
 White-eyed, *148*
 Yellow-green, *151*
 Yellow-throated, *150*
Vulture
 Black, 35, 42, 52, *69*
 Turkey, 35, 42, 45, 49, *68*, 73, 78

Warbler
 Audubon's, 35, (48), 51, 158, *159*, 161, 166
 Black-and-white, 39, *152*
 Blackburnian, *161*
 Blackpoll, *162*
 Black-throated Blue, *158*
 Black-throated Gray, *160*
 Black-throated Green, *161*
 Blue-winged, *153*
 Canada, *165*
 Cape May, *208*
 Chestnut-sided, *162*
 Colima, xi, 32, (47), 49, 50, 132, *154*
 Golden-cheeked, *208*
 Golden-winged, *153*
 Grace's, *161*
 Hermit, *161*
 Hooded, 35, *165*
 Lucy's, 35, *156*

MacGillivray's, 35, *163*
 Magnolia, *158*
 Mourning, *163*
 Myrtle, (48), 51, *158*, 159
 Nashville, *153*
 Olive, *157*
 Olive-backed, *208*
 Orange-crowned, (48), 51, *153*
 Palm, *162*
 Parula, 35, 52, *156*
 Pine, *208*
 Prothonotary, *152*
 Red-faced, *208*
 Townsend's, 35, 52, 159, *160*, 162
 Virginia's, *154*
 Wilson's, 35, *165*
 Worm-eating, *152*
 Yellow, *157*
 Yellow-throated, *208*
Waterthrush
 Louisiana, *163*
 Northern, 35, *163*
Waxwing
 Cedar, 35, (48), 52, *145*
Whimbrel, *87*
Whip-poor-will, (47), 49, 50, *101*
Widgeon
 American, 35, 52, *65*
Willet, *88*
Woodcock
 American, *86*
Woodpecker
 Acorn, 28, 36, 45, (46), 49, 50, 52, *111*
 Downy, *207*
 Golden-fronted, *111*
 Hairy, *207*
 Ladder-backed, 35, 40, 42, (44), 45, 49, 51, *113*
 Lewis', *112*
 Red-headed, *111*
Wren
 Bewick's, 36, (46), 49, 50, 51, *132*
 Cactus, 36, 42, (43), 45, 51, *133*
 Cañon, 36, 42, 45, (46), 49, 50, 51, *134*
 Carolina, 52, *132*

House, 35, 51, *131*
Long-billed Marsh, 35, 52, *133*
Rock, 36, 42, 45, 51, *134*
Short-billed Marsh, *133*
Winter, 52, *132*

Yellowlegs
  Greater, *88*
  Lesser, *88*
Yellowthroat, 35, 41, 42, 52, *164*, 203